PARTY WALLS

PARTY WALLS

Sarah Hannaford
and
Jessica Stephens

RICS BOOKS

Please note: References to the masculine include, where appropriate, the feminine.

Published by RICS Business Services Limited
a wholly owned subsidiary of
The Royal Institution of Chartered Surveyors
under the RICS Books imprint
Surveyor Court
Westwood Business Park
Coventry CV4 8JE
UK

ISBN 1 84219 152 7

Typeset in Great Britain by Columns Design Ltd, Reading
Printed in Great Britain by Bell & Bain, Glasgow

Contents

Contents

Contents

Preface

It is axiomatic that, while chartered surveyors do not need the *breadth* of understanding of the law of their opposite numbers in the legal profession, in a number of key areas of application to property and construction they need a similar *depth* of legal knowledge. Exactly what the key areas may be depends to some extent on the nature of the surveyor's practice. Two obvious examples are the law of landlord and tenant and town and country planning. There are plenty of surveyors who know more about the law relating to rent reviews or compulsory purchase compensation (as well as procedural and valuation aspects) than the average lawyer in general practice.

So surveyors need law and, for a variety of reasons, need to maintain and develop their understanding of it. Changing trends or individual variations in clients' requirements mean that from time to time even the best practitioners (perhaps especially the best practitioners) will feel the need to expand their knowledge. The knowledge acquired at college or in studying for the Assessment of Professional Competence (APC) has a limited shelf life and needs to be constantly updated to maintain its currency. Even specialists working in their areas of expertise need a source of reference as an aide-mémoire or as a first port of call in more detailed research.

The Case in Point Series

RICS Books is committed to meeting the needs of surveying (and other) professionals and the Case in Point series typifies that commitment. It is aimed at those who need to upgrade their legal knowledge, or update it, or have access to a good first reference at the outset of an inquiry. A particular difficulty is the burgeoning of reported decisions of the courts. The sheer scale of the law reports, both general and specialist, makes it very hard even to be aware of recent trends, let alone identify the significance of a particular decision. Thus it was decided to focus on developments in case law. In any given matter, the practitioner will want to be directed efficiently and painlessly to the decision that bears upon the matter he or she is dealing with, in other words to – the Case in Point.

The books in the Case in Point series offer a wealth of legal information which is essential in its practical application to the surveyor's work. The authors have the level of expertise required to be selective and succinct, thus achieving a high degree of relevance without sacrificing accessibility. The series is developing incrementally and will form a collection of specialist handbooks which can deliver what busy practitioners need – the law on the matter they are handling, when they want it.

Party Walls, Sarah Hannaford and Jessica Stephens

The law relating to party walls is a classic example of the kind of area the Case in Point series is intended to cover. It is at once highly specialised and yet of growing importance.

The law itself is complex and extensive. Beyond the statutory framework, which could not itself be described as user-friendly, is a daunting combination of applied property law and obligations and decisions specifically on the party wall legislation, of which over 40 are dealt with in this book. The website of the Pyramus and Thisbe Club, the body of professionals committed to the study and practice of party wall surveying, identifies the original impetus to form the Club as widespread misunderstanding of the case of *Gyle-Thompson v Wall Street (Properties) Ltd* on the validity of notices and awards.

And yet, however little encouragement to exploration by non-experts the technical difficulty of the subject provides, it cannot be ignored by those engaged in property development, construction and property management.

The *Party Wall etc. Act* 1996 has extended to the whole country a legislative regime previously confined to London (and Bristol). The density of urban development alone ensures that the physical relationship between properties will routinely come into question, especially where construction is undertaken. The process may be contentious and the friction acute.

While the role of the party wall surveyor can only be undertaken by a professional with the requisite experience, surveyors in general practice, as well as quantity and building surveyors – not to mention architects, engineers, lawyers and their property owner or developer clients – cannot avoid the need for an adequate understanding of the party wall regime.

To produce a book that could be of use to party wall surveyors themselves, as a supplement to their body of knowledge, and also to these other practitioners, including those from other disciplines, was a major challenge.

The authors, Sarah Hannaford and Jessica Stephens, are barristers at Keating Chambers, one of the country's leading construction law sets. Both have strong practices in party wall disputes and related matters. Their principal achievement in producing this welcome addition to the Case in Point series is the provision of a legal source with sufficient quality of analysis to be useful to the party wall surveyor and sufficient clarity to be accessible to a person who is not an expert in the field. They have met the challenge.

Anthony Lavers, 2004.
Professional Support Lawyer, White & Case, London.
Visiting Professor of Law, Oxford Brookes University, Oxford.
Consultant Editor, Case in Point Series.

Introduction

Until relatively recently, only those living in London and Bristol needed to concern themselves with legislation relating to party walls. Subject to the vagaries of the common law on party walls, rights of support and weatherproofing, those living elsewhere in England and Wales were relatively free to do what they wished with the walls separating their property from that of their neighbours.

As a result of the enactment of the *Party Wall etc. Act* 1996, no landowner can carry out works to his property which might affect a neighbouring property without first complying with the provisions of the Act. However, Parliament has not been alone in making law that encourages adjoining owners to behave in a more 'neighbourly' fashion. The common law also appears to be moving in that direction, following the Court of Appeal decision in *Holbeck Hall Hotel* in 2000. In this case, the Court of Appeal introduced the concept of a measured duty of care or 'reasonableness between neighbours' to determine the respective rights and obligations between adjoining owners.

In many statutes, the devil is in the detail. In this Act, it is in the 'etc' in the title. The Act applies to works to all party structures, including traditional party walls, party fence walls (walls that separate land rather than buildings) and to any other structures (including floors and partitions) that separate buildings or parts of buildings.

The Act's requirements are of particular importance to a modern surveyor's practice. Surveyors need to understand when the Act applies, and what must be done in order to ensure that a client complies with the Act. Non-compliance with the Act can have disastrous consequences. Not only is there the potential for damage to be caused to an adjoining property, there has recently been an indication (in the *Roadrunner* case in the Court of Appeal) that the Courts will take a dim view of a party's failure to comply with the Act. The Court of Appeal took what Lord Justice Chadwick described as a 'robust approach to causation' in this case and found a party who had failed to comply with the Act liable for damage suffered by another, despite the absence of conclusive evidence that the works carried out by that party actually caused the damage.

The Act also gives surveyors the power to determine any disputes that arise between adjoining owners under the Act, subject to an appeal to the County Court. Disputes between neighbours can often become highly sensitive and acrimonious. Given that the Act has opened up an entirely new arena for potential disputes between neighbours, it is vital that surveyors are properly equipped with the knowledge to enable them to make appropriate awards. This book aims to provide all surveyors with the knowledge and understanding of both the procedures laid down by the Act and the legal principles behind it that are necessary to allow them to practice effectively in this area.

The introductory chapter sets out the works and structures to which the Act applies. The second chapter deals with the procedural matters with which parties must comply in order to benefit from the rights the Act confers on property owners. Of vital importance is the proper service of notices. Crucial issues include the content and timing of the notice and the party or parties, by whom and on whom, it must be served. Mistakes in this area can be fatal and have, over the years, been the subject of a number of decided cases.

Chapter 3 is concerned with the dispute resolution procedure. It covers the appointment (and replacement) of surveyors to resolve the dispute. It also deals with the making of an award and, in particular, with which matters are within the scope of the surveyor's jurisdiction. The question of jurisdiction is of critical importance. A surveyor's award is only valid insofar as it deals with matters within the surveyor's jurisdiction. All surveyors must have an understanding of which matters are within their jurisdiction in order to avoid potentially lengthy and expensive disputes as to the validity of the award.

Chapter 4 deals with the effect of an award and the means by which an award can be enforced or challenged. Financial matters, including the apportionment of expenses between the adjoining owners, are considered in Chapter 5. Chapter 6 covers the other rights and obligations that the Act gives to the owners, including the right to access adjoining property to carry out the works, as well as the obligations to make good damage, not cause unnecessary inconvenience and to pay compensation.

Chapter 7 is concerned with the role and liability of party wall surveyors. As will be seen, they are unlikely to have immunity from liability for negligence in awards made under the Act.

Chapter 8 discusses a party's remedies if the building owner has failed to comply with the provisions of the Act. Works which are not sanctioned by an award or agreement made in accordance with the Act are liable to be stopped by order of the Court. As mentioned above, the decided cases tend to show that the Courts take a firm stance where the provisions of the Act have been disregarded.

Chapter 9 deals with the situation where there is a change in ownership of either (or both) of the properties concerned.

The common law of support has progressed significantly over the last few years. An important related development has been the expansion of party wall legislation to the whole country. Party wall awards will inevitably consider support (although not the question of whether easements of support exist). At the same time, the Courts have tried to improve on the limitations of the traditional, and somewhat old-fashioned, common law of support. The traditional common law is still of application, however, for example, where the Act is not complied with. Chapter 10 is concerned with these recent developments.

List of Acts and abbreviations

The following Acts are referenced in this publication. Where an Act is mentioned frequently, it is referred to by the abbreviation that follows the name of the Act in brackets.

Access to Neighbouring Land Act 1992 (**'the 1992 Act'**)
Arbitration Act 1889
Arbitration Act 1950
Arbitration Act 1996
Bristol Improvement Act 1840
Bristol Improvement Act 1847 (**'the 1847 Act'**)
Building Act 1984
Housing Grants, Construction and Regeneration Act 1996
Interpretation Act 1978
Landlord and Tenant Act 1954
Law of Property Act 1925
Local Government Act 2000
London Building Act 1894 (**'the 1894 Act'**)
London Building Act 1930 (**'the 1930 Act'**)
London Building Acts (Amendment) Act 1939 (**'the 1939 Act'**)
Metropolitan Building Act 1855
Party Wall etc. Act 1996 (**'the 1996 Act'**)
Prescription Act 1832
Rent Act 1977

The text of this publication is divided into commentary and case summaries. The commentary is enclosed between grey highlighted lines for ease of reference.

Table of Cases

Table of Cases

1
Application of the *Party Wall etc. Act* 1996

1.1 INTRODUCTION AND BACKGROUND

The *Party Wall etc. Act* 1996 provides a statutory regime governing the relationship between adjoining owners and regulating certain building work carried out on or near to the boundary between adjoining properties. It covers both domestic and commercial property. The 1996 Act came into force on 1 July 1997.

Prior to the commencement of the 1996 Act, the law in relation to party walls and related issues was, with the exception of the London area and Bristol, subject to the common law. Within the London area, there had been a series of statutory codes commencing in the aftermath of the Great Fire of London in 1666 and culminating in Part VI of the *London Building Acts (Amendment) Act* 1939. The 1996 Act provides a similar scheme to the 1939 Act and extends this to the whole of England and Wales. The 1939 Act and the *Bristol Improvement Act* 1847 were repealed when the 1996 Act came into force.

The 1996 Act permits building owners to carry out works to a party structure or in the vicinity of an adjoining owner's building which could otherwise constitute a nuisance or trespass. It also safeguards the interests of the adjoining owner, for example, by requiring notice of works to be given and the building owner to make good damage.

1.2 STRUCTURES TO WHICH THE 1996 ACT APPLIES

The term with which everyone is familiar is a 'party wall'. The 1996 Act, however, applies to three types of structure: party walls, party fence walls and party structures. They are all defined in section 20 of the Act.

1.2.1 **Party wall**

There are two types of party wall.

- The first type is a wall that forms part of a building and stands on lands of different owners to a greater extent than the projection of any artificially formed support on which the wall rests.
- The second type of wall is defined as so much of a wall (not being the first type of wall) that separates buildings belonging to different owners.

The second type of wall will only be a party wall to the extent that it separates two buildings. Therefore, a wall that separates two buildings for one storey, but above that storey is simply the external wall of one building (and does not stand on the land of both owners) will not be a party wall above first-storey level. Likewise, a wall that separates houses for the full depth of one house but then extends back as the external wall of the second house (and stands only on the land of that owner) will not be a party wall beyond the back of the first house.

Weston v Arnold (1873)

The plaintiff and the defendant in this case owned properties that were separated for the first storey by a wall. There was no dispute that, for the first storey, the wall was a party wall. Above that height, the plaintiff's wall continued and had windows in respect of which the plaintiff had acquired rights of light by prescription. The defendant argued, under the *Bristol Improvement Acts* 1840 and 1847, that the whole wall was a party wall, so that the defendant was entitled to erect a building that obstructed the plaintiff's light. The Court held that the first storey of the wall was a party wall. However, the wall above that level was not a party wall, but simply the external wall of the plaintiff's property.

Drury v Army and Navy Auxiliary Co-Operative Supply Ltd (1896)

A provision of the *London Building Act* 1894 required warehouses, above a certain size, to be divided by party walls.

Parts of the building were to be five storeys high, while others were to be only one storey in height. It was held that a wall that was a party wall because it divided adjoining buildings or, as here, divided portions of a warehouse, was not a party wall at a height above which it stopped fulfilling that function.

London, Gloucestershire and North Hants Dairy Co v Morley & Lanceley (1911)

This case also dealt with the 1894 Act. The wall in question separated the parties' premises up to a certain height. Above that height, the Dairy had raised the height of the wall. Morley & Lanceley (M & L) wanted to raise the wall further. They served notice and obtained an award from surveyors entitling them to do the works, on the basis that the whole of the wall was a party wall. The Court decided that the wall was a party wall so far as it separated buildings. The upper part of the wall was therefore not a party wall and M & L were not entitled to raise it higher.

1.2.2 **Party fence wall**

A party fence wall does not form part of a building. It is a wall used or constructed for separating the land of two owners and stands on the land of both owners.

1.2.3 **Party structure**

A party structure is defined as a party wall and also a floor, partition or other structure separating buildings or parts of buildings approached solely by separate staircases or entrances.

1.3 **WORKS TO WHICH THE 1996 ACT APPLIES**

There are three types of work covered by the 1996 Act:

- the construction of party structures on or at a boundary where there is no existing party structure (section 1 works);
- works to existing party structures (section 2 works); and

3

- excavations within six metres of other buildings or structures (section 6 works).

1.3.1 Work where there is no existing party structure (section 1 works)

Section 1 of the 1996 Act applies (see section (1)(a)) where the boundary is not built on at all. It also applies (see section (1)(b)) where there is a boundary wall, unless this is a party fence wall or the external wall of a building. The external wall of a building will be a party wall if it stands on the land of both owners, but not otherwise. This section therefore excludes party walls, party fence walls and the external walls of a building standing on the land of one owner only. In such cases, section 2 applies.

Section 1 contemplates two different types of work. First, the building owner may wish to build a wall standing on both lands (i.e., a party wall or a party fence wall – see section 1(2)). Second, he may wish to build a wall wholly on his own land (see section 1(5)). In either case, the building owner must serve a notice on the adjoining owner at least one month before he intends the work to start.

The first type of wall may, however, only be built with the consent of the adjoining owner. With his consent, the wall may be built half on the land of each of the respective owners, or in any other agreed position. The cost will be shared between the owners, from time to time, having regard to the use each owner makes of the wall (see section 1(3)). If the adjoining owner does not consent, the building owner may only build wholly on his own land and at his own expense (section 1(4)).

Where the building owner wishes, or is obliged as a result of lack of consent, to build a wall wholly on his own land, he has the right to build the wall at his own expense at any time between one and 12 months of the date of the notice (section 1(6)). He also has the right to place projecting footings and foundations below the level of the adjoining owner's land, if this is necessary for the construction of the wall (section 1(6)) and subject to providing compensation for any damage occasioned by building the wall or by placing footings on the adjoining land (section 1(7)). 'Special' foundations, which are defined as foundations in which an assemblage of beams or rods is employed to distribute load (section 20) can, however, only be constructed with consent (see section 7(4)).

1.3.2 Work where there is an existing party structure (section 2 works)

Section 2 of the 1996 Act applies where there is already a party structure at the boundary. It also applies, in certain circumstances, to external walls of a building (other than party walls) and to arches or other structures connecting buildings (see sections 2(2)(a), (d), (g), (h) and (j)).

With two exceptions, before exercising any section 2 right, the building owner must serve a 'party structure notice' on the adjoining owner at least two months before the proposed works are due to begin (sections 3(1) and (3)). The exceptions are, first, where the adjoining owner agrees to the proposed works, and second, where the proposed works are carried out in order to comply with a notice served on the building owner under a statutory provision relating to dangerous or neglected structures (see 2.1 below).

The works permitted include underpinning, raising or repairing party structures; reducing the height of party walls; cutting into, or cutting projections away from, walls and structures; and repairing party structures and the building owner's own walls. The works can be divided into three broad categories:

- works necessary due to defects or want of repair;
- works to structures that do not conform with statutory requirements; and
- works that the building owner wishes to carry out for his own purposes.

1.3.2.1 Defects or want of repair

Works necessary to resolve defects or lack of repair in party structures are specifically dealt with in section 2(2)(b) of the

1996 Act. Section 2(3) makes it clear that section 2(2)(a) can also apply in such situations. The latter section applies both to party structures and the building owner's own external wall.

Whether there is a defect or want of repair will depend on the purpose for which the wall is used. Something that amounts to a defect or lack of repair in a wall separating two houses will not necessarily be a defect in a party fence wall.

Barry v Minturn (1913)

This case considered whether dampness was a defect for the purpose of a similar provision under the 1894 Act. A wall divided two gardens. On the building owner's side, it was used as the retaining wall of an extension to her house. On the adjoining owner's side, it was used as a garden wall. The building owner wanted to carry out works from the adjoining owner's side to rectify the dampness and sought a party wall award to this effect. The surveyors decided that the wall was not so defective or out of repair as to require work under an award. The House of Lords considered that dampness was not a defect unless its existence rendered the wall less effective for its intended use. Dampness in a garden wall would therefore be immaterial. However, the wall was defective in so far as it allowed water into the building owner's house. The building owner was therefore entitled to carry out work from her side of the wall to prevent damp ingress, but not from the other side.

1.3.2.2 **Non-compliance with statutory requirements**

Sections 2(2)(c) and (d) of the 1996 Act deals with structures, partitions and arches or structures connecting buildings over ways or passages belonging to others that do not conform to statutory requirements. The building owner is entitled to demolish and rebuild such structures so as to conform with statutory requirements.

A structure built before 18 July 1996 (the date on which the 1996 Act was passed), which conformed with statutory requirements current on the date on which it was built, is deemed to conform with statutory requirements (section 2(8)). This appears to mean that the right to demolish and rebuild structures dating from before 18 July 1996 is limited to those that did not conform with statutory requirements when they were built. However, curiously, for structures built after 18 July 1996, it appears that the right exists in relation to both those that did not conform when built and those that subsequently became non-conforming, due to the introduction of new statutory requirements.

1.3.2.3 Works for the building owner's own purposes

The remainder of section 2(2), as well as section 2(2)(a) (which can apply whether or not there are defects in the party structure) allows a building owner to carry out works on his own account that affect existing party structures, walls and buildings. These works include underpinning; cutting away projections; cutting into a wall; and raising and lowering the height of a wall. The right to carry out such works is generally subject to the obligation to make good and, in the case of sections 2(2)(a), (e) and (m), to carry out other ancillary works.

Section 2(2)(e): Rebuilding the wall

Section 2(2)(e) entitles a building owner to demolish and rebuild a party structure that is of insufficient strength or height for the purposes of his intended building. The building owner may rebuild to a lesser height or thickness where the rebuilt structure is of sufficient height and strength for the adjoining owner's purposes. However, it seems that the building owner has no right to make other changes to the form of the structure.

Burlington Property Company Ltd v Odeon Theatres Ltd (1939)

Surveyors appointed to make an award under a similar provision of the *London Building Act* 1930 allowed the building owner to rebuild a party wall, so that instead of containing the original three windows, it had door openings. The Court of Appeal decided that the surveyors had no jurisdiction to allow a building surveyor to alter the form of the wall in this respect. [The 1930 Act did not allow rebuilding to a lesser height or strength, as is permitted by the 1996 Act. Nonetheless, it seems likely that the 1996 Act (like the 1930 Act) would not permit the sort of alteration in form that occurred in *Burlington*.]

Section 2(2) of the 1996 Act contains two important changes from the previous law, relating to reducing the height of party structures and weatherproofing.

Section 2(2)(e) and (m): Reducing the height of the wall

Gyle-Thompson v Wall Street (Properties) Ltd (1974)

This case was decided under the 1939 Act. The building owner wished to demolish and rebuild the party wall to a reduced height. Under the 1939 Act, sections 46(a) and (k) allowed a building owner to demolish and rebuild a party wall. The Court decided that this required reconstruction to the same height.

Now, however, sections 2(2)(e) and (m) of the 1996 Act allow a building owner to reduce the height of the party wall. This right is limited. Under section 2(2)(e), the lesser height must be of sufficient strength and height for the purposes of the adjoining owner. The right under section 2(2)(m) is limited by section 11(7), which entitles the adjoining owner to serve a counter-notice requiring the building owner to maintain the existing height of the wall, subject to paying a proportion of the costs.

Section 2(2)(n): Weatherproofing

If an owner of a terraced property demolishes his property, this can leave the adjoining owner's house exposed to the weather and, therefore, liable to damage. Prior to the 1996 Act, however, claims by adjoining owners in this situation did not always succeed.

The 1939 Act did not require a party who demolished his property, leaving the adjoining owner's half of the party wall exposed, to weatherproof the exposed wall. The position at common law was no better. No right to protection from the weather exists, although in some cases the Courts managed to find a remedy for adjoining owners.

Phipps v Pears (1964)

The plaintiff and the defendant in this case owned adjoining properties. The plaintiff's property had been built up against the defendant's house, but was not bonded to it and did not rely on it for support. The defendant's property was neglected and the local authority ordered the defendant to demolish it. This was done, leaving the flank wall of the plaintiff's property exposed. The plaintiff's exposed wall then became saturated with rain and suffered frost damage. The plaintiff claimed damages. The Court of Appeal held that there was no easement of protection from the weather known to the law. The plaintiff was therefore left without a remedy for the weather damage.

Bradburn v Lindsay (1983)

The plaintiff and the defendant owned semi-detached houses. The defendant allowed her house to become neglected and the local authority eventually demolished it. The plaintiff's property, as a result, suffered from loss of support, exposure to dry rot and the weather. The Court decided that, as there was an easement of support and this was a party wall, the plaintiff was entitled to have his house weatherproofed.

Rees v Skerrett (2001)

The plaintiffs and defendant owned adjoining terraced houses separated by a party wall. The defendant was served with notices by the local authority which required him to demolish his building and to shore up and weatherproof the adjoining building. The defendant carried out the demolition works, but failed to provide adequate shoring or protection for the exposed wall. The Court of Appeal decided that, although there was no easement of protection against the weather as decided by *Phipps v Pears*, the defendant, who had been required to weatherproof by the local authority,

9

owed the plaintiffs a duty of care to prevent or minimise the risk of damage to their exposed wall. The plaintiffs were therefore entitled to damages for damage by the weather.

These problems have now been resolved. Section 2(2)(n) of the 1996 Act does now require a building owner who exposes a party structure to provide adequate weathering. An adjoining owner now has a remedy against a building owner who fails to do so, without the need to rely on the rather uncertain state of the common law in relation to weatherproofing.

1.3.2.4 Special foundations

Special foundations are dealt with separately by the 1996 Act. Section 20 defines 'special foundations' as foundations in which an assemblage of beams or rods is employed for the purpose of distributing load.

A building owner who wishes to use special foundations must serve a party structure notice giving full particulars of the details of the proposed special foundations, including plans, sections, details and reasonable particulars of the loads to be carried (section 3(1)(b)).

A building owner may not place special foundations on an adjoining owner's land without the latter's consent in writing (section 7(4)). The adjoining owner may serve a counter-notice imposing his own requirements as to the strength and depth of the foundations (section 4(1)(b)).

1.3.3 Excavations (section 6 works)

Section 6 of the 1996 Act does not relate to party structures. Instead, it applies to excavations, whether or not for the purpose of erecting a building or structure, within six metres of the adjoining owner's building or structure. Within such a distance, excavations could adversely affect the adjoining owner's foundations.

There are two types of work to which the section applies.

- The first is where the building owner wishes to carry out an excavation within three metres of any part of a building or structure of an adjoining owner and the excavation will extend to a lower level than the bottom of the adjoining owner's foundations (section 6(1)).
- The second, set out in section 6(2), is where the building owner wishes to excavate within six metres of any part of a building or structure of an adjoining owner. In this case, the Act applies if any part of the excavation, within the distance of six metres, will meet a plane drawn downwards towards the excavation at an angle of 45 degrees from the line formed by the intersection of:
  - the plane of the level of the bottom of the adjoining owner's foundations; and
  - the plane of the external face of the external wall of the adjoining owner's building or structure.

Essentially, this means that the Act applies between three and six metres from the adjoining owner's building or structure, where the intended excavation is to a depth below the bottom of the adjoining owner's foundations that exceeds the distance between the excavation and any part of the adjoining owner's building or structure.

The two situations are illustrated in the diagram overleaf.

In both cases, the building owner must serve notice one month prior to the intended commencement of works. The building owner may, or may be required to, underpin or strengthen the foundations of the adjoining owner's building at his own expense (section 6(3)).

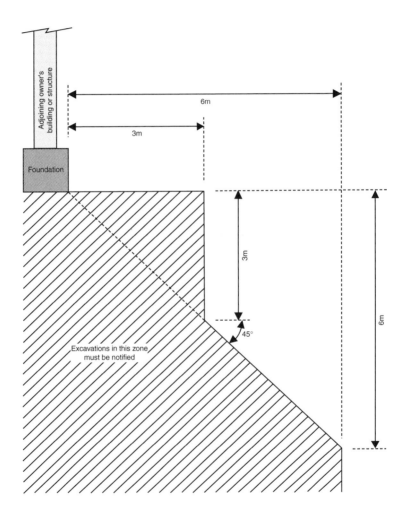

2
Notices and owners

2.1 WHEN ARE NOTICES REQUIRED TO BE SERVED BY A BUILDING OWNER?

A notice is required to be served by a building owner whenever he proposes to carry out any works under sections 1, 2 or 6 of the *Party Wall etc.* Act 1996. A notice in connection with section 2 works is called a party structure notice.

Notices must be served:

- for section 1 works, at least one month before the building owner intends to commence the works (sections 1(2) and (5));
- for section 2 works, at least two months before the building owner intends to commence the works (sections 3(2)); and
- for section 6 excavations, at least one month before the building owner commences excavation works (section 6(5)).

A building owner is not required to serve a party structure notice (for section 2 works) if consent in writing has been obtained from all adjoining owners and occupiers (section 3(3)(a)), or before complying with any notice served under any statutory provisions relating to dangerous or neglected structures (section 3(3)(b)).

Sections 61–65, London Building Acts (Amendment) Act 1939

These sections (extended to include the outer London boroughs by the *Local Government Act* 2000) give local authorities in London the power to serve notices on owners and/or to apply to a Magistrates' Court for an order in relation to dangerous and neglected structures.

Sections 77–79, Building Act 1984

These sections give local authorities outside London similar powers in relation to dangerous and neglected structures.

If a dangerous structure notice requires a building owner to demolish a wall, but makes no requirement as to rebuilding, this does not entitle the owner to rebuild it without having first obtained a party wall award under the 1996 Act.

Spiers & Son Ltd v Troup (1915)

The plaintiffs in this case served a party wall notice on the defendant under the *London Building Act* 1894. However, before an award was made, they exposed the party wall. A magistrate's order was made which required the plaintiffs to demolish the wall, as it considered it a dangerous structure, but made no requirements for rebuilding it. The plaintiffs rebuilt it without waiting for a party wall award and then claimed a contribution to the expenses of rebuilding it from the defendant under the Act. The magistrate's order related only to pulling down the wall. The plaintiffs had failed to comply with the Act in relation to the rebuilding, in that they had done so without a party wall award. They could not for this reason, among others, claim expenses under the Act.

2.2 WHAT SHOULD BE INCLUDED IN A BUILDING OWNER'S NOTICE?

The 1996 Act briefly describes what should be included in a notice. The requirements are slightly different in each case. For section 1 works, the notice must indicate the building owner's desire to build, and must describe the intended wall (sections 1(2) and 1(5)). For section 2 works, the notice must include the name and address of the building owner, the nature and particulars of the proposed work, including details of any special foundations, if applicable, and the date on which the proposed work will begin (section 3(1)). For section 6 excavations, the notice must indicate the building owner's proposals and state whether he proposes to underpin or otherwise strengthen or safeguard the adjoining owner's foundations (section 6(5)). Section 6(6) also requires the notice to be accompanied by plans and sections showing the site and depth of the excavation and the site of any building or structure the building owner intends to erect.

It is suggested that it would be sensible for the notices to give the relevant information as fully and clearly as possible. Standard forms for the notices are contained in the RICS guidance note, *Party Wall Legislation and Procedure*. A notice must be sufficiently clear to enable the adjoining owner to understand the works to be carried out and to decide whether or not he wishes to consent.

Hobbs, Hart & Co v Grover (1899)

The plaintiff and the defendant owned properties separated by a party wall. The defendant intended to pull his property down and rebuild it. However, the notice he served failed to specify the particulars of the proposed work and simply quoted parts of the relevant Act. The Court's view was that a notice must be sufficiently clear and intelligible as to enable the adjoining owner to see what counter-notice should be given. The defendant therefore had to serve an amended notice before he could start his proposed works.

Spiers & Son Ltd v Troup (1915)

The notice served described the proposed works as pulling down and rebuilding the party structure if, on survey, it were found so defective or out of repair as to make such operation necessary or desirable, and to perform all other necessary works incidental thereto. The judge considered this to be very vague and hypothetical and insufficient to comply with the requirements of the 1894 Act.

2.3 HOW SHOULD A NOTICE BE SERVED?

2.3.1 Methods of service

Section 15 of the 1996 Act sets out the requirements for valid service of a notice. A notice must be served in one of the following ways:

- by delivering it in person;
- by sending it in the post to the person's last known residence or place of business in the UK;
- in the case of a company, by delivering or posting it to the secretary of the company at its registered or principal office; or
- if a notice is to be served on an owner, by addressing it to 'the owner' of the named premises and delivering it to a person at the premises or, in the absence of any person at the premises, by fixing it to a conspicuous part of the premises.

Fax and e-mail are not valid methods of service in accordance with section 15.

2.3.2 Service by post

Service by post is not restricted to first class post. Second class post, registered or recorded delivery will therefore also be permissible.

Interpretation Act 1978, section 7

Section 7 of this Act provides that service is deemed to be effected by properly addressing, pre-paying and posting a letter containing the document and, unless the contrary is proved, to have been effected at the time at which the letter would be delivered in the ordinary course of post.

However, if the contrary is proved, for example, by return of the letter undelivered by the Post Office, it will not be treated as duly served.

R v London County Quarter Sessions Appeals Committee ex parte Rossi (1956)

A Court official sent notice of a hearing to the respondent by registered post. That notice was returned with a note from the Post Office stating that there had been 'no response'. The Court of Appeal decided that where a notice had been returned undelivered, proper service had not been effected.

It seems that the last known residence or place of business will be the place last known to the sender of the notice, although the address may have changed and others may know of the new address.

Austin Rover Group Ltd v Crouch Butler Savage Associates (1986)

The plaintiff issued a writ and served it by first class post to the last address of the defendant known to the plaintiff. However, three months earlier the defendant had moved without the plaintiff's knowledge. The Court of Appeal considered that the 'last known' address meant the address last known to the plaintiff (although the case was in fact decided on a different point).

2.4 BY WHOM AND ON WHOM MUST A NOTICE BE SERVED?

Notices are served by and on 'owners'. Mere occupiers, not falling within the definition of owners, have no right to send or receive notices.

2.4.1 Who is an owner?

Section 20 defines owners to include three categories, listed below.

(1) A person in receipt of, or entitled to receive, the whole or part of the rents or profits of land.

This is aimed primarily at the freehold owner and any leaseholders not in possession (i.e., those who have sub-let the property). It does not include a person who receives, or is entitled to receive, rent as an agent for another person (such as a receiver).

Solomons v R Gertzenstein Ltd (1954)

The definition of owner under the 1930 Act was held by the Court of Appeal not to include a receiver who had been appointed by the building society under the mortgage and collected the rents as agent for the mortgagor. The wording of the Act did not include an agent. It seems that this would also apply to the 1996 Act.

(2) A person in possession of land, otherwise than as a mortgagee, or as a tenant from year to year or for a lesser term, or as a tenant at will.

This is aimed at leaseholders who are in possession, except for the excluded categories. Tenants for periods of one year or less (for example, monthly or weekly tenants) and tenants at will are all expressly excluded. Mortgage companies are also expressly excluded.

It was decided in a case under the *London Building Acts (Amendment) Act* 1939, that statutory tenants are not included in the statutory definition of 'owner'. A statutory tenancy is a right provided by the *Rent Act* 1977 to a tenant, in certain circumstances, who continues to occupy a property after the expiration of the contractual tenancy period. It is a personal right of occupation and not a tenancy in the usual sense. The same case also decided that the tenants must have a legal (rather than an equitable) interest in the property to qualify as owners. (A legal lease is any lease created by deed or a lease where the tenant is in possession, is for a term in excess of three years and is for the best rent obtainable.)

Frances Holland School v Wassef (2001)

Mr and Mrs Wassef were statutory tenants, for the purposes of the *Rent Act* 1977, of premises that adjoined the School's premises. The School wanted to construct a new building, access to which required the demolition of a building that adjoined Mr and Mrs Wassef's premises. The judge decided that Mr and Mrs Wassef were not adjoining owners (under a similar provision of the 1939 Act). He decided that owners who were tenants were limited to those who held legal interests in land of a duration greater than one year and did not include statutory tenants.

(3) A purchaser of an interest in the land under a contract for purchase or under an agreement for a lease, otherwise than under an agreement for a tenancy from year to year or for a lesser term.

The third category was introduced by the 1996 Act. A person who has not yet completed a purchase of land, but has exchanged contracts, is now an owner. This means that, between exchange of contracts and completion, the vendor and purchaser will both be owners, as the vendor will fall into either the first or second category and the purchaser into the third category.

2.4.2 On whom must a notice be served?

A notice must be served on 'the' adjoining owner (section 1 and 2 works) or 'any' adjoining owner (section 6 works). The difference in wording does not alter the meaning. In any case, as illustrated further below, a building owner may need to serve notice on more than one person or party.

Section 20 of the 1996 Act defines an adjoining owner as any owner of land, buildings, storeys or rooms adjoining those of the building owner and, for the purposes of section 6, within three or six metres (as relevant) of the proposed excavation.

In re Ecclesiastical Commissioners for England's Conveyance (1936)

'Adjoining' land, not in the specific context of party walls, was held by the Court of Appeal to mean land that touched the land it was said to adjoin.

In the context of party walls, the 'adjoining' land, buildings, storeys and rooms will include those on the other side of the party wall or within three or six metres of the excavation. Adjoining may have a wider definition than in the Ecclesiastical Commissioners case – for example, where the building owner owns a flat. In such a case, work may affect other flats on either side of the party wall. These flats may not actually touch the building owner's flat (although they will

19

touch the party wall), but are likely to fall within the definition of 'adjoining' under the 1996 Act.

More than one person may come within the definition of 'adjoining owner'. For example, if the adjoining property is leased, there will be a freehold and a leasehold owner. Likewise, where contracts have been exchanged for the sale of the adjoining property, the vendor and the purchaser will both be adjoining owners. Where several people fall within the definition of the 'owner' of an adjoining property, the notice must be served on all of them (despite the fact that a building owner will not necessarily acquire knowledge of a contract to purchase the adjoining owner's property). There is an exception to the need to serve all people in the category of adjoining owner. The exception occurs when a class of people hold a joint interest, for example, as joint tenants, in which case it is sufficient to serve a notice on one of that class.

Crosby v Alhambra Co Ltd (1907)

The plaintiffs' premises, which were sub-let to the council, were separated by a party wall from the defendant's premises. The defendant intended to carry out works affecting the party wall and served notice under the relevant Act on the council, but not on the plaintiffs. The plaintiffs applied for an injunction to prevent the works proceeding. It was held that the defendant was required to serve a party wall notice on every person falling within the definition of 'owner' under the relevant Act, except that, where there was a class of persons entitled to a particular interest in the adjoining premises, such as joint tenants or tenants in common, it was only necessary to serve notice on one of that class. The Court made a declaration that the defendant was not entitled to proceed without first serving the notices on the plaintiffs.

The building owner is not required to serve notice on adjoining tenants who do not fall within the definition of 'owner' under section 20 of the 1996 Act. No notice needs to be served on tenants for terms of one year or less, statutory tenants and, it seems, those who do not have a legal interest in the property (see 2.4.1 above).

Frances Holland School v Wassef (2001)

The Court considered the question of whether the defendants, Mr and Mrs Wassef, as statutory tenants of the adjoining premises, were 'owners' for the purposes of the 1996 Act. It was held that Mr and Mrs Wassef were not adjoining owners and the plaintiff School was not obliged to serve the defendants with a notice. The Court stated that the definition of 'owner' was limited to those who held legal interests in land of a duration greater than one year. This did not include statutory tenants.

It is not advisable to serve a notice on the adjoining owner's surveyor rather than the adjoining owner himself. If the surveyor is not authorised to accept service, there is a risk that any resulting party structure award will be invalid.

Gyle-Thompson v Wall Street (Properties) Ltd (1974)

The defendant (the building owner) served party wall notices on Mr Johnson, the plaintiffs' surveyor. Mr Johnson did not send these notices to the plaintiffs, as he thought that the defendant had done so. The plaintiffs maintained that Mr Johnson had no authority to accept service. The judge decided that there was insufficient evidence that Mr Johnson had been held out as the plaintiffs' agent for the purposes of service of the notices. He therefore decided that the notices, and the resulting award, were invalid (for this, among other reasons).

2.4.3 **By whom must a notice be served?**

The notice must be served by the building owner. Section 20 of the 1996 Act defines the building owner as an owner of land who is desirous of exercising rights under the Act. The definition of owner is set out in 2.4.1 above.

As with adjoining owners, there may be more than one building owner. However, the owner who must serve the notice is the owner who is desirous of exercising rights under the 1996 Act. This means, for example, that if the leasehold owner wishes to carry out the works, only he need serve the notice. The freehold owner does not also need to do so.

Loost v Kremer (1997)

The defendant (the leasehold owner) wished to carry out works of extension to his property, which would affect the party wall between his premises and the plaintiff's property. The defendant had served a party structure notice. The freehold owner had not joined in such a notice or served her own notice. She had, however, given her permission for the works to be carried out and allowed a variation to the lease to that effect. The plaintiff objected to a subsequent party structure award on the ground, among others, that the freehold owner had not served a notice and should have done, as she was a building owner. The judge decided that she was not a building owner, as the person who was desirous of doing the works was the leasehold owner. The freehold owner therefore did not need to serve a notice.

On the other hand, where people own a joint interest in a property, all of them must serve the notice as building owners. A joint interest will be in one 'layer of ownership' (i.e., the freehold or the leasehold). This means that where a leaseholder wishes to do building work and the leasehold is in joint names (that is, there are joint tenants), all joint tenants must serve the notice. The same applies where the freehold is in joint names. This is different from the position in relation to service of notice on adjoining owners (see 2.4.2 above).

Lehmann v Herman (1993)

The defendants, Mr and Mrs Herman, owned a long lease of a flat in property separated from the plaintiffs' premises by a party wall. The defendants proposed to carry out certain works and a party structure notice was served by Mr Herman only. The judge decided that the notice was invalid as it had been served by only one of two joint tenants. He considered that, in the case of joint tenants, it could not be said that only one of them occupied or was in possession of the flat. He accepted the argument that a building owner must mean the owner of any layer of ownership (such as the freehold layer or the leasehold layer), but decided that the building owner included everyone within that layer.

A person is not entitled to serve a notice as building owner before he has exchanged contracts for a lease of property, as he does not fall within the definition of 'owner'.

Spiers & Son Ltd v Troup (1915)

The freehold owner of a terraced house had agreed with the plaintiff that the latter would demolish and rebuild his property and then be granted a lease of the property. The plaintiff, before signing the building agreement, before going into occupation of the property and without having any agreement for a lease, served a party wall notice on the adjoining owner. The judge held that the plaintiff was not a building owner, as it did not fall within the definition of 'owner' and was therefore not entitled to serve the notice.

2.4.4 Failure to serve a notice properly

It is important to ensure that notices are properly served by and on the correct parties. A failure properly to comply with the obligation to serve a notice is likely to render any subsequent award invalid and incapable of enforcement. The adjoining owner may apply for an injunction to prevent the work going ahead or a declaration that the building owner is not entitled to proceed without serving proper notice. In such a case, the process will have to be restarted by the service of a compliant notice and repeated to produce an award that properly authorises the carrying out of the proposed works.

Gyle-Thompson v Wall Street (Properties) Ltd (1974)

The defendant building owner served notices on the plaintiffs' surveyor and not the plaintiffs. The judge did not consider that the plaintiffs' surveyor had authority to accept service. He therefore decided that the surveyor's award, which had arisen from the incorrectly served notice, was invalid. For this reason, and as a result of other defects in the procedure and the award, the judge held that the plaintiffs were entitled to an injunction to prevent the works going ahead. The judge emphasised the importance of proper compliance with the relevant Act (the 1939 Act), as follows:

> 'ss 46 et seq of the 1939 Act give a building owner a statutory right to interfere with the proprietary rights of the adjoining owner without his consent and despite his protests. The position of the adjoining owner, whose proprietary rights are being compulsorily affected, is intended to be safeguarded by the surveyors appointed pursuant to the procedure laid down by the Act. Those surveyors are in a quasi-judicial position with statutory powers and responsibilities. It therefore seems to me important that the steps laid down by the Act should be scrupulously followed throughout, and that short cuts are not desirable.'

Lehmann v Herman (1993)

The defendants were joint tenants who both had a leasehold interest in their property. As a result of the notice being served on behalf only of Mr Herman and not his wife, the judge decided that the party structure notice was invalid and that the plaintiffs were entitled to a declaration to that effect.

Patsalides v Foye (2002)

A party structure notice was not served properly in accordance with the 1996 Act. A notice, falsely dated 5 July 2001, was faxed to the adjoining owner's surveyor (who had no authority to receive such a notice) over a month later. The award was signed two days afterwards. It was held that the surveyor's 'award', which falsely recited the date of service of the structure notice, was invalid.

The judge in *Gyle-Thompson* raised the possibility of an adjoining owner waiving, or being estopped from relying on, a defect in the notice. Waiver or estoppel could result from agreement or conduct. For example, if the adjoining owner made it clear that he knew about the irregular service of the notice and was happy to continue with the procedure, he might have waived the invalidity of the notice or be estopped from relying on it. However, it is obviously advisable to ensure that the notices are correctly served, rather than hope to rely on arguments of waiver or estoppel, which may be difficult and expensive to prove in court. The question of waiver and estoppel has been considered in the context of the appointment of a surveyor in *Loost v Kremer* (see 3.2 below).

2.5 THE ADJOINING OWNER'S RESPONSE

The provisions relating to the consent or dissent of the adjoining owner differ between the three types of work to which the 1996 Act applies.

If a building owner wishes to build a wall under section 1 on both lands, he needs written consent within 14 days of service of the notice (sections 1(3) and (4)). If he does not receive such consent, he can only build a wall wholly on his own land. Although the building owner must serve a notice, there is no requirement for consent if the building owner either chooses, or is obliged, to build a wall wholly on his own land.

For section 2 works, the adjoining owner has a number of options. Firstly, he can serve a notice of consent within 14 days of service of the party structure notice. Secondly, he can dissent (although there is no need for him to do so, as, if he does not consent, he is deemed to have dissented (section 5)). Thirdly, he can serve a counter-notice (sections 4 and 11(7)). A counter-notice must be served within one month of service of the party structure notice.

The purpose of a counter-notice is for the adjoining owner to require additional works to be carried out. He may require certain works, such as chimney breasts, piers, and so on, to be built in for his convenience (section 4(1)(a)), although he must pay for such works (section 11(9)). Or, if he agrees to special foundations, he may require these to be deeper or stronger than proposed by the building owner (section 4(1)(b)). If the building owner wishes to reduce the height of a wall under section 2(2)(m), the adjoining owner may require the building owner to maintain the existing height, subject to paying a proportion of the costs of the extra height (section 11(7)). The building owner is obliged to comply with a counter-notice unless it would be injurious to him, or cause him unnecessary inconvenience or delay (section 4(3)).

For section 6 works, if an adjoining owner does not serve a notice within 14 days after service of the building owner's notice indicating his consent to it, he is deemed to have dissented from the notice.

2.6 TIME LIMITS

There are time limits within which works must be commenced.

For section 1 works, the only time limit relates to a building owner building on his own land who places foundations on the adjoining owner's land. The building owner must carry out this work between one month and 12 months of the date of service of the notice.

For section 2 and section 6 works, the building owner's notice will cease to have effect:

- if the work has not begun within 12 months after the date of service of the notice; and
- if the work is not prosecuted with due diligence.

2.6.1 Beginning the work within the 12-month period

Where there is a dispute between the owners, it will be necessary for the surveyors to resolve it by making a party structure award. This, of course, may take some time, particularly if either party then appeals to the Court. It seems, therefore, that the notice will not cease to have effect if the party structure award has not been made, or the appeal has not been heard, within the 12-month time limit.

Leadbetter v Marylebone Corporation (1905)

The defendant building owners served notice of intended works on the plaintiffs. Disputes arose and were referred to the surveyors to make an award. The relevant Act was the 1894 Act, under which the time limit was six months. Before the surveyors had made their award, the six-month period expired. The plaintiffs claimed that the defendant could not proceed with the works and would have to serve a new notice. The Court of Appeal considered that the six-month time period was intended to apply to works in relation to which no dispute arose. It did not therefore apply where surveyors had been appointed to make an award. The defendant was therefore entitled to proceed with the works.

On the other hand, in situations where there is no reason why the building owner should not commence works within the 12-month time period, and, having failed to do so, subsequently tries to commence works after the expiry of that period, an adjoining owner might, in appropriate circumstances, be entitled to obtain an injunction to prevent the building owner from commencing the works.

Awards often set out a period within which works must be commenced. In such a case, if a building owner tried to commence works thereafter, an adjoining owner could, in appropriate circumstances, apply to the Court for an injunction to prevent the building owner going ahead with works at a later date, on the basis that the building owner no longer had statutory authority to do so.

2.6.2 Prosecuting the works with due diligence

Due diligence is essentially a requirement to proceed with reasonable speed.

Greater London Council v The Cleveland Bridge and Engineering Co Ltd (1984)

It was considered in this case (although not required to be finally decided) that 'due diligence' was an obligation on the contractors to execute the works with such diligence and expedition as were reasonably required in order to meet the key dates and completion date in the contract.

The sanction that the notice ceases to have effect if the works are not prosecuted with due diligence is a curious provision. It is difficult to see that a Court would grant an injunction that had the effect of leaving works partly completed. This would often not benefit the adjoining owner, as, for example, his property may be inadequately supported or exposed to the weather. If the notice ceased to have effect, then the surveyors, who derive their jurisdiction from the notice, would cease to be validly appointed.

A more appropriate sanction for delay would be an obligation on the building owner to compensate the adjoining owner for the inconvenience and other costs incurred by the delay. Such a claim could be made under sections 7(1) or (2) of the 1996 Act.

Jolliffe v Woodhouse (1894)

The defendant served notice under the *Metropolitan Building Act* 1855 that he wanted to pull down and rebuild the party wall. The plaintiff claimed that he had taken an unreasonable time to complete the works and was awarded damages by the judge. The Court of Appeal upheld the judge's decision, considering that a building owner had a duty to rebuild with reasonable speed or in a reasonable time. The basis of this claim is not entirely clear from the judgment, although one of the appeal judges referred to the defendant's obligation under the Act not to cause unnecessary inconvenience to the adjoining owner.

3
Dispute resolution

3.1   WHEN DOES A DISPUTE ARISE?

Section 10 of the *Party Wall etc.* Act 1996 provides a mechanism for the resolution of disputes. Disputes either specifically arise or are deemed to arise (see, for example, section 5 of the Act). Disputes can arise between owners in respect of any matter connected with any work to which the Act relates (section 10(1)).

The main type of dispute that arises is whether and how the building owner should be entitled to carry out the work that he proposes. In relation to section 2 and section 6 works, such a dispute will be deemed to arise if the adjoining owner does not serve a notice indicating his consent within 14 days of service of the building owner's notice.

Disputes could arise in relation to a number of other issues, such as who should pay for the works, or for making good damage, or as to whether the building owner should put up security before he is entitled to do the works.

3.2   RESOLVING A DISPUTE: APPOINTMENT OF SURVEYORS

Disputes are resolved by one or more surveyors. There is a choice of two procedures. In the first, the parties can agree on the appointment of one surveyor. Alternatively, the parties can each appoint their own surveyor, who will then select a third surveyor (referred to below as the 'three-surveyor procedure').

The appointment of a surveyor and the selection of the third surveyor must be done in writing (section 10(2)). A failure to appoint a surveyor properly in writing is likely to mean that any award made by the surveyors will be invalid and that the building owner will not be entitled to carry out the works permitted by the award.

Gyle-Thompson v Wall Street (Properties) Ltd (1974)

In this case, there had been two party structure notices and two awards. The adjoining owners' surveyor had not been appointed in writing at all for the purposes of the first notice and award. Written appointments post-dating the award were then signed in order to regularise the fee position. This was prior to service of the second notice. There was no further written appointment of the adjoining owners' surveyor. The judge decided that the adjoining owners' surveyor was not properly appointed in writing for the purposes of the second notice and award. The adjoining owner's surveyor had, nonetheless, been involved in the selection of the third surveyor and the second award had been made by two surveyors, including the third surveyor. It was held that the award was void because the adjoining owners' surveyor was not validly appointed and therefore had no statutory authority to agree to the selection of the third surveyor.

Loost v Kremer (1997)

The judge in this case considered whether the building owner's surveyor had been correctly appointed. He was appointed in writing to serve the relevant notices. The appointment letter, however, said that in the event of a dispute the building owner 'would' appoint the surveyor to act. The party structure notice referred to the appointment of the building owner's surveyor in the same terms. It was argued that this was not a valid appointment. The judge decided that the appointment was a valid conditional appointment. The condition occurred once a dispute arose in relation to the notice. The judge went on to say that, in any event, various letters written by the adjoining owner acknowledging that the surveyor was the building owner's surveyor would amount to a waiver or estoppel, and would prevent the plaintiff from arguing that the appointment was not valid.

If one party refuses to appoint a surveyor, or fails to do so within ten days of a request, the other party is allowed to appoint a surveyor on his behalf (section 10(4)). If one of the surveyors appointed refuses to select a third surveyor, or fails to do so within ten days of a request, the other surveyor can apply to the appointing officer to make the selection (section 10(8)). The appointing officer is the person appointed by the local authority for that purpose (section 20). If, however, the appointing officer or his employer is a party to the dispute, the secretary of state makes the selection (section 10(8)).

3.3 WHO CAN BE A SURVEYOR?

A surveyor is defined in section 20 of the 1996 Act as any person, not being a party to the matter, appointed or selected under section 10 of the Act to determine disputes in accordance with the Act. 'The surveyor' does not need to have any specific qualifications. He may already be involved in the building owner's works, as surveyor, architect or engineer.

Loost v Kremer (1997)

It was argued that the building owner's surveyor could not properly act under the *London Building Acts (Amendment) Act 1939*, as he was acting on behalf of the company of which he was a director, and had a conflict of interest, being the building owner's architect for the works. The judge decided that a surveyor must be an individual, not a company, but that the building owner had, in fact, appointed his surveyor as an individual. The judge also decided that the fact that he was the architect for the works did not prevent him being the surveyor for the purposes of the Act, nor give him a conflict of interest.

3.4 WHEN CAN SURVEYORS BE REPLACED?

3.4.1 Appointment of new surveyors

The parties are not entitled to rescind the appointment of their surveyors or that of the third surveyor (section 10(2)). However, there are certain circumstances in which a new surveyor needs to be appointed, as set out below.

- If an agreed surveyor refuses to act, neglects to act for ten days after service of a request, dies or becomes or deems himself incapable of acting, then the procedure has to begin again (section 10(3)). This means that the parties have to decide whether to agree on another single surveyor or whether to use the three-surveyor procedure.
- Where the three-surveyor procedure is used, a party may appoint another surveyor in place of his original surveyor if the surveyor dies or becomes or deems himself incapable of acting (section 10(5)). There is no provision, in this case, for the procedure to begin again. The new surveyor will therefore continue from where the previous surveyor left off.
- If the third surveyor refuses to act, neglects to act for ten days after a request, dies or becomes or deems himself incapable of acting, the other two surveyors must select a replacement forthwith (section 10(9)).

It seems that in order to entitle a party to appoint another surveyor, the refusal to act must be a refusal to act altogether. A refusal to act in a particular manner is not likely to amount to a refusal to act.

Burkett Sharp & Co v Eastcheap Dried Fruit Co (1961)

This case concerned whether an arbitrator had 'refused to act' for the purposes of section 7 of the *Arbitration Act* 1950. The defendant claimed that the arbitrator had refused to act and tried to appoint another arbitrator in his place. In fact, the arbitrator had refused to act as sole arbitrator in circumstances in which another arbitrator had been appointed. The judge therefore decided that this was not a refusal to act as arbitrator at all, but a refusal to act in a particular manner. It therefore did not amount to a refusal to act.

3.4.2 **Ex parte procedure**

A party to the three-surveyor procedure is not entitled to appoint a new surveyor for himself where his surveyor refuses or neglects to act. (This is different from the position for agreed surveyors or third surveyors – see 3.4.1 above.) When a party-appointed surveyor in the three-surveyor procedure refuses to act effectively or neglects to act effectively for ten days after service of a request, then the other surveyor may act ex parte, as if he were an agreed surveyor. This remedy could seriously penalise the appointing owner of the defaulting surveyor. The other surveyor will therefore need to take great care before deciding that the other party's surveyor has refused or failed to act effectively. If he does so decide, and is wrong, an ex parte award will almost certainly be invalid.

Frances Holland School v Wassef (2001)

Each party to this dispute had appointed a surveyor under the 1939 Act to resolve a dispute about the proposed works. Resolution of various disputes was not achieved over a long period of time. Mr and Mrs Wassef's surveyor considered that the other surveyor was refusing or neglecting to act. He therefore sent a letter in which he gave ten days' notice that he would act ex parte. The School's surveyor wrote two letters in reply, but the Wassefs' surveyor proceeded to make an ex parte award. The judge held that there was no evidence of a refusal or of neglect to act. The judge expressed the view that any surveyor who wished to use the ex parte procedure must comply strictly with the formalities of the Act. The judge considered that for the ex parte award to be valid, it should have set out accurately the grounds on which the surveyor was acting ex parte. The award in this case did not do so. The judge decided that the award was invalid.

This case was decided under the 1939 Act, in which refusals or neglects to act were not qualified by the word 'effectively'. However, it is considered that the result would have been the same under the 1996 Act.

3.5 MAKING OF THE AWARD

Where the agreed surveyor procedure is used, the agreed surveyor determines the dispute by an award (section 10(10)).

Where the three-surveyor procedure is used, there are a number of possibilities.

■ All three or any two of the surveyors may make the award (section 10(10)).
■ Either of the surveyors, or either of the parties, may ask the third surveyor to determine the dispute by award (section 10(11)).
■ Under the ex parte procedure (see 3.4.2 above), one of the party-appointed surveyors may make the award (sections 10(6) and (7)).

3.6 SCOPE OF THE SURVEYOR'S JURISDICTION

Section 10(10):

The appointed surveyors have jurisdiction to make an award in respect of any matter connected with any work to which the 1996 Act relates.

Section 10(12):

The award itself may determine:

● the right to execute any work;
● the time and manner of executing any work; and
● any other matter arising out of or incidental to the dispute, including the costs of making the award.

The jurisdiction of the surveyors appears from the above sections to be broadly defined. However, the Courts have repeatedly refused to allow surveyors to determine matters that are not properly covered by the provisions of the Act or included within the dispute referred to them. If the surveyors go outside their jurisdiction in their award, there is a real risk that the award may be invalid in whole or in part.

Re Stone and Hastie (1903)

A party wall had been raised by the freehold owners of
Mr Hastie's property some years before he became a tenant
of the property. Subsequently, the owner of the adjacent
property, Mr Stone, wished to carry out works on the party
wall. Mr Hastie did not consent to these works and the
surveyors made an award. That award included a decision
that Mr Stone should pay money to Mr Hastie to represent a
proportion of the original costs of the works, as he was now
making use of the party wall (under a provision similar to
section 11(11) of the 1996 Act). Mr Hastie had not incurred
the original costs, as these had been incurred by the freehold
owners. It was held by the Court of Appeal that the
surveyors had no jurisdiction to decide anything beyond the
dispute submitted to them (which related to Mr Stone's new
works to the wall). In addition, the surveyors had no
jurisdiction to award a proportion of the costs of the original
works to Mr Hastie, a subsequent tenant, who was not the
party who had originally incurred the expenses. This part of
the award was therefore invalid.

Gyle-Thompson v Wall Street (Properties) Ltd (1974)

The surveyors made an award permitting the building
owner to demolish a party wall and rebuild it to a lesser
height. Under the 1939 Act, the Court decided that the
building owner had no right to rebuild the wall to a lesser
height and that the surveyors' award was made without
jurisdiction and was therefore invalid. (The building owner
does now have such a right – see 1.3.2.3 above.)

Woodhouse v Consolidated Property Corporation Ltd (1993)

The building owner (the defendant) served a party structure
notice after it had already commenced works. The notice set
out its intention to carry out works to a party wall.
However, before the 14-day period for the adjoining owner
(the plaintiff) to give consent had expired, the wall
collapsed, causing damage to the plaintiff's property. A
third surveyor was appointed and made an award
determining the responsibility for the collapse and

providing that the building owner was to pay the proper cost of reconstructing those parts of the adjoining owner's premises that were damaged as a result of the collapse of the party wall. The Court of Appeal held that the surveyors were only entitled to resolve differences between adjoining owners relating to whether one of them should be permitted under the relevant Act to carry out the works in the notice, and if so, the terms and conditions under which that person was permitted to carry out such works. The surveyors were not entitled to determine other disputes between the parties. The collapse of the wall was not within the Act or the party structure notice and had been made outside the third surveyor's jurisdiction. The award was therefore invalid.

A question that has arisen is whether surveyors have jurisdiction to make awards in relation to future rights or obligations of the parties. It is suggested that it is not desirable for awards to provide rights or obligations going beyond the proper completion of the works to the party structure. It has, however, been held in one case that a continuing obligation to weatherproof is enforceable, although not to be recommended.

Leadbetter v Marylebone Corporation (1904)

The plaintiff wished to carry out works to the party wall and served a party structure notice on the defendant. A dispute arose as to the works to be done and was resolved by a surveyors' award. However, the surveyors, in their award, also gave the defendant the right to raise the wall at any time in the future. Some time later, the defendant decided that it wanted to raise the wall and tried to do so without serving a further party structure notice, on the basis that it was entitled to do so by the terms of the award. The Court of Appeal decided that the surveyors only had jurisdiction to determine matters within the notice in respect of which they were appointed. They did not have jurisdiction over every dispute that might arise between the parties. The part of their award that permitted the defendant to raise the wall at any time in the future was therefore made without jurisdiction and was invalid.

Marchant v Capital & Counties plc (1983)

The plaintiff owned a house which had been built onto the back of a large warehouse owned by the defendant. The defendant decided to demolish the warehouse. This would have the effect of leaving the previously internal wall of the plaintiff's property unsupported and exposed to the weather. The three surveyors therefore made an award obliging the defendant to provide support to the wall and to maintain the exposed face of the wall in a weatherproof condition. The works were carried out. Some years later, damp appeared inside the plaintiff's house, having penetrated through the party wall. The plaintiff commenced proceedings against the defendant. The Court of Appeal rejected the argument that it was outside the surveyors' jurisdiction to impose a continuing obligation on the defendant. It held that the surveyors' award in this case imposed a continuing obligation on the defendant to maintain the wall in a weatherproof condition. It did, however, caution that it may in practice be undesirable for surveyors to impose continuing obligations by an award rather than providing for the carrying out of works that would have a long-term result.

3.7 INTERFERENCE WITH AN EASEMENT

Section 9 of the 1996 Act provides that nothing in the Act shall authorise any interference with an easement of light or other easements in or relating to a party wall.

One of the main easements that may affect a party wall is an easement of light. Even if a party wall award appears to authorise it, a building owner is not entitled to carry out works that would interfere with an easement of light. If a party wall award in fact authorises interference with an easement of light, it will not be enforced. In such a case, the adjoining owner may be able to obtain an injunction to prevent the work going ahead. The existence of an easement of light is not a matter that party wall surveyors should decide.

Crofts v Haldane (1867)

The defendant had served notice under the relevant Act and built a wall in accordance with the award of the three surveyors. The plaintiff started proceedings for an injunction, claiming that the wall interfered with his rights of light. The plaintiff's claim succeeded. The Court rejected the argument that the dispute as to the right of light should be determined by the surveyors. The Court considered that as the building owner had no right to raise a party wall so as to interfere with the right to light, there was nothing under the Act in relation to which the surveyors could make an award.

The position with easements of support is slightly more complicated. Party wall surveyors will deal with issues of support in the award, as works to a party wall will often involve the temporary removal and replacement of adequate support. If the works authorised by the award are not adequate, this is not likely to emerge until a later stage. At this stage, the adjoining owner may need to claim compensation under section 7(2) (see 6.1.3.1 below), or may wish to claim against the surveyors (see 7.2 below).

3.8 AN AWARD AS TO COSTS

The surveyors have jurisdiction to include a provision as to costs in the award. Section 10(13) of the 1996 Act provides that the reasonable costs incurred in making or obtaining the award, including any reasonable inspections of work, shall be paid by such of the parties as the surveyor making the award determines.

This provision makes it clear that the surveyors have jurisdiction to order one or other of the parties to pay the costs. It is less clear from the words whether the provision entitles the surveyors to allocate the costs between the parties, as arbitrators may, in accordance with section 59 of the *Arbitration Act* 1996. Nonetheless, it seems likely that section 10(13) does give the surveyors the discretion to order the costs to be shared between the parties.

3.9 SUCCESSIVE AWARDS

Section 55(i) of the 1939 Act provided that the surveyor(s) could settle by award any matter to which a notice related or was in dispute from time to time during the works. The wording in section 10(10) of the 1996 Act is slightly different. It now provides that:

> 'The agreed surveyor or as the case may be the three surveyors or any two of them shall settle by award any matter–
>
> (a) which is connected with any work to which this Act relates, and
> (b) which is in dispute between the building owner and the adjoining owner.'

It seems that the intention of the new wording is, as with the 1939 Act, that the surveyors are to be entitled to settle different disputes as and when they arise. However, the wording is not entirely clear. In order to ensure that there can be no objection to successive awards, it would be sensible for the surveyors to obtain their instructing owner's agreement to the making of more than one award, should this be necessary. This would be an additional safeguard beyond the common practice of reserving the right in the first award to make further awards.

3.10 CARRYING OUT WORKS BY AGREEMENT

There is nothing to prevent owners agreeing that work may be carried out under sections 1, 2 or 6 of the 1996 Act. This is expressly provided for by section 1(3), section 3(3)(a) and section 6(7). In order to carry out section 2 works, the written consent of both adjoining owners and occupiers is necessary (section 3(3)(a)). Consent from adjoining occupiers is not necessary for section 1 or section 6 works.

Where works are carried out by consent, the parties' surveyors will often reach an agreement rather than make an award. The surveyors will need to ensure that they have each obtained written authority from their instructing owner before attempting to enter into an agreement, to ensure that any such agreement is binding on the owners.

Patsalides v Foye (2002)

The defendant building owner wished to build an extension to his property against the claimant's flank wall. A party structure notice was not served properly in accordance with the 1996 Act. A notice falsely dated 5 July 2001 was faxed to the adjoining owner's surveyor, who had no authority to receive such notices, over a month later. Two days after the faxed notice, the two surveyors signed a document entitled 'Party Structure Award'. The judge decided that this was not a valid award, as no notice had been served. It was also argued that the surveyors had been authorised to *agree* the works to be carried out and that the 'award' was in fact an agreement. However, the judge decided that the adjoining owner's surveyor only had authority from his instructing owner to agree boundaries and corrective action, and not to agree what was set out in the 'award'. He found that both surveyors thought they were making an award, not an agreement. There was therefore no binding award and no binding agreement.

4
Awards – effect, enforcement and challenge

4.1 WHAT IS THE EFFECT OF AN AWARD?

An award is conclusive (section 10(16) of the *Party Wall etc. Act* 1996).

Selby v Whitbread & Co (1917)

The defendant demolished and rebuilt his property further back than its previous position, leaving the front of the flank wall of the plaintiff's property unsupported. A second party wall award required the defendant to provide a pier to support the front part of the plaintiff's wall. The defendant did not appeal the award. However, it tried to oppose enforcement of the award on a number of grounds, one of which was that the provision of a pier was unnecessary. The Court held that, as the defendant had not appealed the award, it could not object to its enforcement on the basis that the surveyors had been wrong to decide that a pier was necessary. The award was conclusive.

The conclusiveness of an award is subject to the following:

- an appeal (see 4.3 below);
- a challenge to the validity of the award (see 4.4 below); and
- the fact that an award cannot authorise infringement of an easement (see 3.7 below).

4.2 WHAT CAN A PARTY DO TO FORCE THE OTHER PARTY TO COMPLY WITH AN AWARD?

Awards may include the following:

■ authorisation to the building owner to carry out certain works, which will often include works to safeguard the adjoining owner's property;

■ an obligation on the adjoining owner to provide access for the building owner to carry out certain works (see 6.2 below); or

■ payment by one owner of a sum of money to the other.

If one owner does not comply with his obligations under the award, the question is whether and how the other owner can force compliance.

4.2.1 Works for the benefit of the adjoining owner

In appropriate circumstances, an adjoining owner could obtain an order from the Court forcing the building owner to carry out the works that he is required by the award to carry out for the benefit of the adjoining owner. A similar application to the Court could be made if the building owner failed to carry out the works in accordance with the terms of the award – for example, if the building owner built the wall to an unauthorised height or in an unauthorised place. In such a case, the adjoining owner might wish to apply to the Court for an injunction to prevent the building owner from doing so, or, if necessary, for an injunction to remove unauthorised work. An order requiring a building owner to comply with an award would probably be in the form of an injunction (although it has been described as specific performance – see below). A Court will sometimes order damages instead of an injunction, if it considers that damages are an adequate remedy (see 8.3 below).

Marchant v Capital & Counties plc (1983)

The party wall award in this case stated that the building owner, who wished to demolish his own property, had liberty to carry out certain works to support and to maintain in a weatherproof condition the external wall of the adjoining owner's property. Some 13 years later the adjoining owner started an action, complaining that her property was damp. The building owner argued that he had no obligation to carry out works to remedy the problem, as the award said that he had 'liberty' to do them. The Court of Appeal rejected this argument, stating that the award would be pointless if the building owner could chose whether or not to carry out the works to the adjoining owner's property. The Court held that the building owner was obliged, even years later, to maintain the wall in a weatherproof condition, and made a declaration that the building owner should now do so.

Selby v Whitbread & Co (1917)

The defendant building owners were ordered by a party wall award to provide a pier to support part of the plaintiff's flank wall and to do various other works to the roof and parapets, and so on. The defendant failed to do any of these works. The judge decided not to order specific performance of the obligations in the award, as he considered that damages would be an adequate remedy. He therefore awarded damages for the cost of remedial works and the diminution in value as a result of the lack of support of the flank wall.

4.2.2 Access

The rights of entry enjoyed by a building owner and the surveyors are dealt with in section 8 of the 1996 Act (see 6.2 below). It is a criminal offence not to allow access in certain circumstances. However, it seems likely that if the adjoining owner refuses to provide access, despite the surveyors having included this in their award, the building owner could also apply to the Court for an injunction to force the adjoining owner to comply with the award. Obtaining an order for access under the *Access to Neighbouring Land Act* 1992 would also be a possibility, although the circumstances in which this applies are limited (see 6.2).

4.2.3 Award for the payment of money

If the award provides for payment of a sum of money by one party (for example, for the cost of part of the works) and the other owner does not pay, then the party claiming money could enforce payment in court. Section 17 of the 1996 Act specifically provides that any sum of money payable in pursuance of the Act (other than by way of a fine) is recoverable summarily as a civil debt. This means that the money can be recovered by issuing a complaint in the Magistrates' Court. The payment of a sum due could also be pursued by an action in the County or High Court. Unless the other owner appeals against the award, or it is invalid for jurisdiction reasons, it should be possible to pursue the claim relatively swiftly by applying for summary judgment.

4.3 CHALLENGE – BY WAY OF APPEAL

4.3.1 The nature of an appeal

Either party may appeal against the award within 14 days. The appeal is to the County Court, which may rescind or modify the award and make orders as to costs as it thinks fit (section 10(17)). It has been decided, in relation to the *London Building Acts (Amendment) Act* 1939, that the Court will be able, at the hearing of the appeal, to reconsider the evidence available to the surveyors and, if appropriate, to consider new evidence. The Court will therefore be able to reach its own decision. It seems that the position will be the same under the 1996 Act.

Chartered Society of Physiotherapy v Simmonds Church Smiles (1995)

It was held by the official referee that, given the Court's wide powers under the 1939 Act to rescind or modify an award, it must have the power to re-examine the evidence (factual and expert) and consider new evidence, if appropriate. The Court could then substitute its own findings for the findings of the surveyors.

4.3.2 Time limits for appeals

The 14-day time limit runs from the date on which the award is served on the party who wishes to appeal (section 10(17)).

Service of the award must be in accordance with section 15 of the 1996 Act. This section authorises service by actual delivery, by post or (although this is not likely to be relevant to the service of the surveyors' award) by fixing it to the property.

Interpretation Act 1978, section 7

According to section 7 of the *Interpretation Act* 1978, where an Act authorises or requires a document to be served by post, service is deemed to be effected by properly addressing, pre-paying and posting a letter containing the document and, unless the contrary is proved, to have been effected at the time at which the letter would have been delivered in the ordinary course of post.

Civil Procedure Rules 1998, Rule 6.7

For Court documents, the *Civil Procedure Rules* (CPR) introduced dates by which service would be deemed to occur. In the case of first class post, the deemed date of service is the second day after posting. No date is provided for second class post.

Consignia plc v Russell Sealy (2002)

The Court of Appeal decided that, for employment tribunals, it was legitimate to adopt the approach in Part 6.7 of the CPR to service by first class post. Therefore, if a letter was sent by first class post, the Court considered that it would be legitimate to conclude that, in the ordinary course of post, it would be delivered on the second day after it was posted (excluding Sundays, Bank Holidays, Christmas Day and Good Friday, being days when post is not normally delivered).

It is therefore possible that the Courts would use the same approach to service under the 1996 Act. Part 7 of the CPR also gives guidance for personal service and service by delivering the document to or leaving it at a permanent address. In the case of personal service, the document is deemed to be served on that day, except if served after 5 pm on a business day or any time on a Saturday, Sunday or Bank Holiday. If a document is delivered or left at a permanent address, it is deemed to be served on the following day.

Under the CPR, it has been decided that evidence of earlier receipt of a document will not override the date that is deemed in accordance with the Rules.

Godwin v Swindon Borough Council (2002)

A limitation period expired on Friday 8 September. The claimant posted the Court claim forms on Thursday 7 September. The defendant received them on Friday 8 September, but claimed that they were served out of time. It was held by the Court of Appeal that the claim form was served out of time because the deemed date of service was two days later – i.e., the following Monday. The deemed date of service could not be contradicted by evidence of the date of actual service.

It is not possible for a time limit set by any Act of Parliament to be extended by the Court.

Riley Gowler Ltd v National Heart Hospital Board of Governors (1969)

This case concerned an appeal against a party wall award. There was an argument about the date of delivery of the award (which arose on the different wording of the 1939 Act). It was, however, agreed between the parties that the Court could not extend the time set by the Act for appealing.

If the final day of the 14-day period is a Bank Holiday, it is possible that an appeal made on the following day would be in time.

Hodgson v Armstrong (1967)

This case concerned whether or not an application to Court under the *Landlord and Tenant Act* 1954 had been made within the four-month time limit set by the Act. The time limit expired on Easter Monday. An attempt was made to deliver by hand on the Thursday afternoon, but the Court was shut until the Tuesday. On the Tuesday, the application posted on the Thursday arrived in the post. The Court of Appeal confirmed that it could not extend a time limit set by an Act of Parliament. However the Court decided that, where the last day allowed by the Act was a Bank Holiday, the Act should be construed with the effect that an application that arrived at the Court on the following day was within time.

It is also possible that an appeal could be made after expiry of the 14-day period, if both parties agree that this can be done.

Kammins Ballrooms Co Ltd v Zenith Investments (Torquay) Ltd (1970)

This case also concerned whether an application to the Court under the *Landlord and Tenant Act* 1954 had been made within the time limits, although this time the question was whether it had been made prematurely (the Act providing that it must be made not less than two and not more than four months after the tenant's request). The House of Lords decided that the parties could agree that an application to the Court could be made, even though the notice had not been served in accordance with the time limit in the Act. On the facts of the case, however, they decided that there had been no such agreement, nor had the time limit been waived.

4.4 CHALLENGE – WHERE THE AWARD IS INVALID

An award which is invalid (for example, if it was made without jurisdiction or in excess of jurisdiction – see 3.6 above) is not conclusive and cannot be enforced. An award that authorises interference with an easement is also invalid and cannot be enforced (see 3.7 above). Such awards do not need to be the subject of an appeal to the County Court. A party can therefore object to their enforcement after expiry of the 14-day time limit for appeal.

Gyle-Thompson v Wall Street (Properties) Ltd (1974)

The plaintiffs claimed that the party wall award that authorised the rebuilding of a wall to a lesser height than its previous height was invalid, as it was not within the surveyors' jurisdiction under the 1939 Act. It was argued that the plaintiffs' only remedy was to appeal to the County Court. The judge rejected this argument. He considered that a party did not need to appeal to the County Court in order to free itself from an award that had been made outside the surveyors' jurisdiction.

It is possible that only part of an award may be invalid. In such cases, where that part can be severed from the rest of the award without substantially affecting or altering the rest of the award, it should be possible to enforce the unaffected parts.

Selby v Whitbread & Co (1917)

The defendant argued that part of a party wall award that required the defendant to build a pier to support the plaintiff's wall was invalid. It was also argued that, if part of the award was invalid or void, this meant that the whole award was invalid. The judge did not accept this and considered that an award could be enforced in part, provided that the good could be separated, with reasonable clarity, from the bad. This would not be possible where the void part was inextricably connected to the remainder. The judge did not consider that any part of this award was invalid or void.

However, he also considered that, on the facts of this case, the obligation to build the pier could, if necessary, have been separated from other parts of the award, such as the obligations to repair the roof and to carry out work to the parapet.

4.5 OTHER METHODS OF CHALLENGE

Awards can only be challenged by way of appeal or on grounds of invalidity. Therefore, although the temptation to obstruct the works or to use other methods of self-help may exist, such acts could amount to trespass or a nuisance for which the adjoining owner could be liable.

Hyde Housing Association v Tate (2000)

Mr Tate had, according to the Court of Appeal, been 'at war' with the Housing Association over an extension to the adjoining terrace house. In spite of the party wall award, he repeatedly obstructed works and attacked the new structure with a pickaxe. The Court of Appeal stated that the only proper method of challenge was by way of the appeal process and not by using self-help. Mr Tate was liable to the Association for trespass and nuisance.

5
Payment for the works

5.1 EXPENSES

'Expenses' is the term used in the *Party Wall etc.* Act 1996 to refer to the cost of carrying out the works. The surveyors have jurisdiction to make an award in relation to the payment of expenses. Expenses are dealt with in detail in section 11 of the Act.

The allocation of expenses between the building owner and the adjoining owner is logical, although on occasion it is necessary to look at more than one section of the Act to work out the rules.

5.1.1 The general rule and exceptions

The general rule is that expenses of work carried out under the 1996 Act are paid by the building owner (section 11(1)). There are, however, a number of exceptions to the general rule, as explained below.

- **Section 1 works – a wall built on both parties' land**

The expenses of a section 1 wall built on both parties' land are to be paid from time to time by the two owners in proportion to the use made by each owner of the wall (sections 1(3) and 11(3)). The contributions of the two owners are assessed by reference to the cost of labour and materials prevailing at the time when use is made by each owner of the wall (section 1(3)).

- **Section 2 works – where necessary, due to defect or want of repair**

Section 2(a) relates to works carried out by a building owner either where the wall is defective or needs repair, or for his own purposes. Section 2(b) relates to works carried out by a building owner on account of defect or want of repair. The expenses of works under these sections that are necessary on account of defect or want of repair are to be paid in proportion to the use which the owners make or may make of the structure concerned and the responsibility of each owner for the defect or want of repair of the structure (sections 11(4) and (5)).

■ **Counter-notices and requests of the adjoining owner**

Where the building owner proposes to reduce the height of the wall under section 2(2)(m) and the adjoining owner serves a counter-notice requiring him to maintain the height, section 11(7) provides that the adjoining owner is to pay a due proportion of the cost of the wall in so far as it exceeds the height allowed by section 2(2)(m).

Where the adjoining owner requests additional works to be carried out (either by a counter-notice under section 4(1)(a) or by some other request), the adjoining owner is obliged to pay for the additional works requested (section 11(9)).

■ **Subsequent use of work**

Where an adjoining owner subsequently makes use of work carried out solely at the expense of the building owner, the adjoining owner is to pay a due proportion of the expenses incurred by the building owner in carrying out that work (section 11(11)). The building owner shall be taken to have incurred expenses calculated by reference to what the cost of the works would have been had they been carried out at the time when that subsequent use was made.

It seems that an adjoining owner will be obliged to pay a proportion of the expenses for the subsequent use of the wall to the original building owner and his successor in title (where the property has been sold), but not to a subsequent tenant of the building owner, where the latter paid for the original works.

Re Stone and Hastie (1903)

A party wall had been raised by the freehold owners of Mr Hastie's property, wholly at their expense, some years before he became a tenant of the property. Subsequently, the owner of the adjacent property, Mr Stone, wished to carry out works to the party wall. Mr Hastie did not consent to these works and the surveyors made an award. As Mr Stone was now making use of the wall, Mr Hastie asked the surveyors to include in their award a sum for the due proportion of the expenses incurred by the freehold owners of his property in building the wall originally. The claim was made under a section of the *London Building Act* 1894, equivalent to section 11(11) of the 1996 Act. The surveyors included such a sum in their award. The Court of Appeal, however, considered that this part of the award was invalid, as the original costs had been incurred by the freehold owners and not Mr Hastie, a subsequent tenant.

Mason v Fulham Corporation (1910)

The plaintiff wished to raise a party wall and served notice to that effect under the 1894 Act. He entered into an agreement with the defendant that if and when the defendant subsequently wished to use the wall, the defendant would pay half of the expenses. This agreement was made to deal with the section of the 1894 Act equivalent to section 11(11) of the 1996 Act. By the time that the defendant wished to use the party wall, the plaintiff had sold his interest in the property. He nonetheless tried to claim half of his expenses from the defendant. The Court decided that he was not entitled to any contribution, as the person entitled to the contribution under the Act was the person who was the building owner at the time when the money had to be paid – i.e., the plaintiff's successor in title.

5.1.2 Special rules for 'special foundations'

If an adjoining owner has consented to special foundations, but later builds on his land and finds that his costs are increased by the existence of the special foundations, the owner of the building to which the special foundations belong must pay the adjoining owner the additional cost, once he receives an account (see section 11(10)). It seems clear that the obligation to pay falls on a subsequent building owner, if the property has been sold since the original works were carried out, by use of the phrase 'the owner of the building to which the special foundations belong'. The reference to the adjoining owner having consented to special foundations, however, indicates that it may only be the original adjoining owner who can claim.

5.2 ACCOUNT FOR WORKS CARRIED OUT

Where a building owner carries out works and the expenses of such works are, either in whole or in part, to be paid by the adjoining owner in accordance with section 11 of the 1996 Act, an account must be served by the building owner on the adjoining owner (section 13). There are two time limits:

- the building owner must serve the account within two months of completion of the works; and
- the adjoining owner may serve notice of any objection to the account within one month of its service.

If the adjoining owner wishes to dispute the amount of the account, he must serve a notice stating his objection within one month of its service. If he does not do so, he is deemed to have no objection. It seems that, if the adjoining owner does not object to a properly served account in time, he will have lost his right to object and must pay the account.

It is less clear from the cases whether a building owner who fails to serve his account during the two-month period will lose his right to be reimbursed by the adjoining owner. It is suggested that, despite the decision in *Spiers & Troup* (see below), the wording of section 13(1) of the 1996 Act does not preclude the building owner from making a claim outside the two-month period.

Spiers & Son Ltd v Troup (1915)

The plaintiffs had served a party wall notice in relation to the demolition and rebuilding of a party wall. However, before an award was made, they exposed the party wall and the council required them to demolish it, as it was considered a dangerous structure. The plaintiffs then rebuilt the wall and claimed a contribution to the expenses of the work from the defendant. The plaintiffs' claim failed for a number of reasons. In relation to the account, it failed for two reasons.

Firstly, the account was not delivered to the defendant within the time limit (which was one month under the relevant Act). The judge decided that the requirement to deliver the account within one month was a condition precedent to a building owner's entitlement to claim payment from the adjoining owner. Secondly, as the plaintiffs had not carried out the work in accordance with the provisions of the Act (as to proper notice and in accordance with a party wall award), they were not entitled to claim a contribution under the Act.

J Jarvis & Sons Ltd v Baker (1956)

In this case, by comparison, the judge did not decide that the service of the account on the adjoining owner was a condition precedent to the building owner's entitlement to a contribution. An award was made for repairs to a party wall pursuant to the *London Building Acts (Amendment) Act* 1939. The award required the adjoining owner to pay half of the costs of the repair works. The account was not served on the adjoining owner for over two years. The judge considered that the adjoining owner was liable to contribute to the account in accordance with the award, despite the fact that the account had not been served in time. However, the adjoining owner was not precluded from challenging the amount of the account, as it had been served out of time.

The building owner must prepare the account by estimating and valuing at fair average rates and prices. This must be in accordance with the nature of the work, the locality and the prevailing cost of labour and materials at the time the works were carried out. The adjoining owner is therefore only liable for a fair price, which is not necessarily the same as the price the building owner actually paid. However, it appears that if the building owner's account claims the actual price (or a proportion of it) rather than the fair price, this will not prevent the building owner from recovering the fair price.

Reading v Barnard (1827)

The building owner submitted an account which set out the details of the actual costs rather than the costs to which he was entitled under the relevant Act. The judge decided that this was sufficient compliance with the Act and that the building owner was entitled to the amount properly calculated in accordance with the Act.

Section 14(2) of the 1996 Act provides that, until the adjoining owner pays for works in accordance with the account served under section 13, the property in such works remains in the building owner. It is not clear how this provision would be enforced against a subsequent purchaser of the adjoining owner's property.

6
Ancillary rights and obligations of the owners and occupiers

6.1 OBLIGATIONS OF THE BUILDING OWNER

6.1.1 Making good damage

The building owner has obligations in certain circumstances to make good damage caused by the carrying out of the works. In all such cases, the adjoining owner is entitled to require, instead, that the expenses of doing such work are determined under section 10 of the *Party Wall etc.* Act 1996 and paid to him instead (section 11(8)).

The building owner's obligations to make good arise in relation to some, but not all, works carried out for the building owner's own purposes under section 2. The obligations arise only in relation to works carried out for the building owner's own purposes (the third category identified in 1.3.2 above). In these cases, the building owner has obligations, as set out in section 2(3)–(6):

- to make good all damage occasioned to the adjoining premises, their internal furnishings and decorations, where works are carried out under sections 2(2)(a), (e), (f), (g) and (h); and
- to make good all damage occasioned to the wall of the existing building when carrying out work under section 2(2)(j).

The building owner also has other specific ancillary obligations in relation to works under sections 2(2)(a), (e) and (m), for example, constructing or reconstructing a parapet (see sections 2(3), (4) and (7)).

In all other situations, the building owner has no obligation to make good. However, it seems that in these other cases the same effect may be achieved under the 1996 Act, as the building owner now has an obligation to pay compensation (see 6.1.3 below).

Video London Sound Studios Ltd v Asticus Ltd (2001)

Under the *London Building Acts (Amendment) Act* 1939, it was decided by a judge in the Technology and Construction Court (TCC) that making good did not include damage to electronic equipment, as this did not fall within the term 'finishings', which was used in that Act instead of the word 'furnishings' now used in the 1996 Act. There is a distinction, used primarily in relation to leases, between 'fixtures' and 'chattels'. Whether an item is a fixture depends on the degree and purpose of its annexation to the property. The judge in this case considered that 'finishings' meant the same as 'fixtures'. Therefore, as the equipment was free-standing and was only attached to the walls for the purpose of connection to the power supply, it was not a fixture. It seems that such electronic equipment would now fall within the term 'furnishings' used in the 1996 Act.

6.1.2 Not to cause unnecessary inconvenience

A building owner is not entitled to exercise any right conferred on him by the 1996 Act in such a manner or at such a time as to cause unnecessary inconvenience to any adjoining owner or occupier (section 7(1)).

The obligation not to cause unnecessary inconvenience will involve consideration of the particular method to be used for carrying out the works.

Barry v Minturn (1913)

A party wall divided two gardens. On the building owner's side, it was used as the retaining wall of an extension to her house. The wall was defective in that it allowed damp to penetrate into the building owner's property. The judge, on an appeal from the award of the surveyors, considered three possible methods of remedying the problem, of which two involved the insertion of a vertical damp-proof course, two inches thick, either on the adjoining owner's side of the wall or in the middle of the wall. The House of Lords upheld the judge's decision in favour of the latter solution, on the grounds that the former would have caused the adjoining owner great inconvenience. They considered that it was not appropriate to direct works that entailed great inconvenience to the adjoining owner, if it were possible to direct other works which, while equally effective and not involving any considerable extra cost for the building owner, would be accompanied by no such inconvenience.

It seems that the obligation to carry out works without causing unnecessary inconvenience will also include an obligation to do so without unreasonable delay.

Jolliffe v Woodhouse (1894)

The defendant served notice under the *Metropolitan Building Act* 1855 that he wanted to pull down and rebuild the party wall. The plaintiff claimed that he had taken an unreasonable time to complete the works and was awarded damages by the judge. The Court of Appeal upheld the judge's decision, considering that a building owner had a duty to rebuild with reasonable speed or in a reasonable time.

The obligation not to cause unnecessary inconvenience will also include taking adequate precautions in relation to the hours of working, noise and dust. The Courts have considered this duty in connection with claims made for nuisance at common law arising from building operations. The principles applicable to party walls under section 7(1) are likely to be similar.

Andreae v Selfridge & Co Ltd (1938)

The plaintiff occupied land from which she operated a hotel. The defendant owned the surrounding land and carried out extensive demolition work on this land for rebuilding purposes. The plaintiff sued the defendant for nuisance arising out of the dust and noise, claiming that she had lost significant custom as a result. The Court of Appeal considered that since building operations cannot be carried out without a certain amount of noise and dust, neighbours have to put up with some degree of discomfort. If building works were reasonably carried on and all proper and reasonable steps were taken to ensure that no undue inconvenience was caused to neighbours, they would not be entitled to complain. However, the defendant in this case had caused noise at unreasonable hours and the quantity of dust and grit was described by the Court as insufferable. The duty was to take proper precautions, to exercise reasonable skill and care and to see that the nuisance was reduced to a minimum. This could include restricting the hours of work or the amount of a particular type of work done at any one time, and using proper technical methods to avoid inconvenience. On the facts of the case, the plaintiff succeeded.

Party wall awards usually stipulate requirements as to hours of work and so on, so as to avoid unnecessary inconvenience. If such obligations are not complied with, an adjoining owner could, in appropriate circumstances, obtain an injunction from the Court to enforce compliance with the award or the 1996 Act. Even if the award does not contain such obligations, an adjoining owner or occupier could, in appropriate circumstances, apply to the Court for an injunction to enforce the building owner's obligations to comply with section 7(1) of the 1996 Act.

6.1.3 To pay compensation

There are three specific obligations to pay compensation. They all provide for compensation not just to the adjoining owners, but also to the adjoining occupiers.

6.1.3.1 Section 7(2)

A building owner is obliged to compensate any adjoining owner or occupier for any loss or damage that may result to them by reason of any work executed under the 1996 Act. This is a new obligation on the building owner, which did not appear in the 1939 Act. There have not yet been any decisions on this section of the 1996 Act.

Compensation under this section is payable by reason of any work executed under the Act. This does not seem to fit in very well with the 'making good' obligations. There is no obligation under section 2 to make good damage occasioned by the work if the work was carried out because of defects or non-conformity with statutory requirements. However, under section 7(2) there is now an obligation to pay compensation instead.

Under the *London Building Acts*, if the work was carried out in accordance with the relevant Act, it was decided that the building owner would avoid liability (other than specific obligations to make good or to avoid unnecessary inconvenience) for loss or damage caused by the carrying out of authorised works. This was the law as stated in *Adams v Marylebone Borough Council* [1907] 2 KB 822.

As a result of section 7(2) of the 1996 Act, this no longer seems to be the case.

It is unfortunately possible in cases where the works have been carried out in accordance with the 1996 Act for damage still to be caused to the adjoining owner's property. This could occur, for example, if the works in the award did not provide adequate support. In such a case, it seems likely that the adjoining owner's remedy against the building owner would be under section 7(2) of the Act, rather than at common law (for example, for an action for loss of support or nuisance). This approach is supported by *Selby v Whitbread* (see below), although in that case there was no question of the award providing for inadequate support.

Selby v Whitbread & Co (1917)

The party wall award required the building owner to provide a pier to support the adjoining owner's premises. The building owner did not do so. The adjoining owner made a claim for the enforcement of the party wall award, but also made an alternative claim for loss of support. The judge made it clear that the *London Building Act* 1894 is a code that substitutes the parties' rights and obligations at common law with rights and obligations under the Act. He considered, therefore, that the correct remedy was for the adjoining owner to enforce the award, rather than to claim for loss of support at common law.

6.1.3.2 Other specific sections requiring compensation

Section 1(7)

A building owner who builds a section 1 wall wholly on his own land is obliged to compensate any adjoining owner or occupier for any damage to his property occasioned by the building of the wall or the placing, under section 1(6), of footings or foundations on his land.

Section 11(6)

A building owner who demolishes a party structure that is of insufficient strength or height for his own purposes under section 2(2)(e) must pay a fair allowance in respect of disturbance and inconvenience to the adjoining owner or occupier.

6.1.4 To protect the adjoining land and premises

Section 7(2) of the 1996 Act requires a building owner, at his own expense, to maintain hoarding, shoring, fans or other temporary constructions for the protection of the adjoining land, building or occupier, where he has laid open any part of the adjoining land or building.

6.1.5 To execute the works properly

Section 7(5) of the 1996 Act requires the building owner to carry out works in accordance with statutory requirements and plans, and with sections and particulars either agreed by the owners or determined by the surveyors. No deviation from such documents is permitted without agreement or determination by the surveyors.

6.2 RIGHTS AND OBLIGATIONS IN RELATION TO ENTRY

Section 8 of the 1996 Act makes provision for rights to enter and remain on any land or premises for the purpose of executing the works during usual working hours. Rights are granted to the building owner and his servants, agents and workmen, and to the surveyors appointed or selected under section 10 of the Act.

In order to exercise such rights, notice must be served on the owners and occupiers of the land or premises (see section 8(3)). Except in cases of emergency, at least 14 days' notice must be given. In cases of emergency, the notice must be such as is reasonably practicable. The methods of serving notice are set out in section 15 of the Act.

The Larchbank (1943)

This case considered the meaning of emergency in the wholly different context of a direction that ships should not use whistles or sirens in a fog except in emergency. The House of Lords defined an emergency as the reasonable apprehension of an immediate danger or the near approach of danger.

The building owner, or his servants, agents and workmen, may remove any furniture or fittings or take any other action necessary for the purpose of executing the works (see section 8(1)). If the premises are closed, the building owner, or his agents or workmen, may, provided that they are accompanied by a police officer, break open any fences or doors to enter the premises (section 8(2)).

The adjoining owners and occupiers are obliged to allow entry. It is a criminal offence for an owner or occupier to refuse to allow the exercise of rights of entry (and other rights under section 8 of the 1996 Act), if that owner or occupier knows, or has reasonable cause to believe, that the person in question is entitled to exercise the rights (section 16). It seems that it would also be possible, in appropriate circumstances, for a building owner to enforce his rights under section 8 by an application to the Court for an injunction.

Access to Neighbouring Land Act 1992

This Act also allows access to neighbouring land and the Court will make an order for access in appropriate situations. However, the rights and the situations in which the Court will make an order are limited to situations in which:

- the person wanting access needs access in order to carry out works reasonably necessary for the preservation of the land; and
- the works cannot be carried out or would be substantially more difficult to carry out without entry on the land.

The Court will not make an order if the owner of the other land, or any other person, would suffer interference with or disturbance of his use or enjoyment of that land or would suffer hardship to such a degree that it would be unreasonable for the Court to make an order.

It was established in *Dean v Walker* (1996) that the *Access to Neighbouring Land Act* 1992 applied to party walls. However, as the rights to enter provided by the 1996 Act are broader than those that can be granted under the 1992 Act, it seems unlikely that it will now be necessary for a party to rely on the 1992 Act where works are needed to a party wall.

6.3 OBLIGATIONS OF BOTH OWNERS TO PROVIDE SECURITY FOR EXPENSES

Section 12 of the 1996 Act makes provision in certain circumstances for either party to serve a notice requiring the other to give security for expenses. Any such notice must be served before the work begins. In the event of a dispute, the entitlement to and amount of any security will be determined by the surveyors.

6.3.1 Security from a building owner

There is no limit on the circumstances in which security may be required from a building owner. Nor are any criteria for the award of security from a building owner provided in the 1996 Act. These issues have not been tested in the Courts.

The entitlement to security seems a sensible method of protecting the adjoining owner from the risk of a building owner starting but not finishing the works. This could cause physical damage to the adjoining owner's property, such as weather damage, as well as financial damage – for example, through an inability to sell the property or a loss of trade.

The security is to be given before the building owner begins any work (section 12(1)). The Act does not spell out that the building owner may not start work without providing the agreed or determined security, and an award requiring security should make this clear. In an appropriate situation, it would be possible to apply to the Court for an injunction to prevent work commencing before the security agreed or determined by the surveyors had been paid.

6.3.2 Security from an adjoining owner

A building owner may only require the adjoining owner to give security in two situations:

- where the adjoining owner has required the building owner to carry out any work, the expenses of which are to be paid in whole or in part by the adjoining owner (i.e., the works set out in a counter-notice served under section 4 and works to which sections 11(7) and (9) of the 1996 Act apply); or
- where an adjoining owner serves a notice requiring the building owner to give security.

It seems sensible for a building owner to be entitled to security from an adjoining owner in the first situation – i.e., for works for which the adjoining owner will eventually have to pay. The logic of the second situation is, however, unclear. This seems simply to be a retaliatory provision for which there is little justification.

There are sanctions if the adjoining owner does not provide the security within one month (section 12(3)). The section is not clearly worded. However, the sanctions appear to be as follows. In the first situation above, the building owner is not required to carry out the works requested by the adjoining owner in his counter-notice. In the second situation, the building owner is not required to provide the security requested by the adjoining owner. The sanction in the second situation seems unfair. The adjoining owner may have real concerns about the building owner's ability to carry out and complete the works and may, therefore, require security. It seems very harsh that if the adjoining owner does not give security himself in such a situation (should the building owner ask for this), that the building owner is likewise not obliged to give such security.

6.4 RIGHTS AND OBLIGATIONS OF ADJOINING OCCUPIERS

An adjoining occupier is defined in section 20 of the 1996 Act as any occupier (as distinct from any owner) of land, buildings, storeys or rooms adjoining those of the building owner and within the distances specified in section 6 of the Act.

Adjoining occupiers (who are not also adjoining owners) have limited rights and obligations. Importantly, the building owner has no obligation to serve a notice of his intention to carry out section 1, 2 or 6 works on an adjoining occupier. However, if the building owner wishes to carry out section 2 works by consent, he needs to have the consent of the adjoining occupiers as well as the adjoining owners (section 3(3)(a)).

The rights and obligations of the adjoining occupiers are as follows.

- The building owner must not exercise any right so as to cause unnecessary inconvenience to adjoining occupiers (section 7(1)).
- Adjoining occupiers are entitled to compensation from the building owner for any loss or damage caused by reason of work carried out in pursuance of the 1996 Act (section 7(2)).
- Adjoining occupiers are entitled to compensation for any damage to their property caused by the building of a section 1 wall wholly on the building owner's land (section 1(7)).

- Hoarding, shoring, fans and temporary constructions under section 7(3) are to be for the security of the adjoining occupiers.
- Adjoining occupiers are obliged to allow entry and so on under section 8 of the 1996 Act, subject to the requirements of notice in that section, and can therefore commit an offence under section 16 if they refuse to permit entry.

The dispute resolution system in section 10 of the 1996 Act does not refer to the appointment of a surveyor by an adjoining occupier (see section 10(1), which refers to disputes between building owners and adjoining owners). It therefore seems likely that the adjoining occupier cannot use the dispute resolution system under section 10 except in the one situation expressly provided for by the Act, which is section 1(8). Under this section, any dispute arising under section 1 between the building owner and any adjoining occupier is to be dealt with under section 10. It seems, however, that the only such dispute that could arise would relate to compensation under section 1(7), as this is the only section in which adjoining occupiers are mentioned.

7
The role and liability of party wall surveyors

7.1 ROLE OF SURVEYORS

In the older cases, judges frequently referred to the surveyors appointed to resolve disputes under the various *London Building Acts* as arbitrators. On occasions, the provisions of *Arbitration Acts* were applied to the procedure under the *Building Acts*. The following cases illustrate this.

Re Stone and Hastie (1903)

An application was made to enforce the award of the surveyors under the *Arbitration Act* 1889, as if the award was an arbitration award. On the appeal, the relevant part of the award was found to be invalid (see 3.6 above), so that the point did not arise.

In re Metropolitan Building Act, ex parte McBryde (1876)

One of the surveyors appointed under the *Metropolitan Building Act* 1855 refused to appoint a third surveyor (on the instructions of his instructing owner). The Court appointed a third surveyor under the provisions of a statute allowing the Court to appoint an arbitrator where one of the parties would not do so. (This would not be necessary under the *Party Wall etc.* Act 1996, as a result of section 10(8) of that Act.) The judge decided that the procedure under the *Building Act* was arbitration and therefore that this statute applied to allow the Court to appoint a third surveyor.

Arbitrations usually arise as a result of agreements between the parties within contracts. A procedure set out in a statute can also be what is known as a 'statutory arbitration'. The

Case in Point – Party Walls

Building Acts, including the 1996 Act, do not state that the surveyors are to act as arbitrators or that the procedure is to be an arbitration. The Courts have not made any decision on this issue since 1876, although more recently a Technology and Construction Court (TCC) judge, considering the *London Building Acts (Amendment) Act* 1939, suggested that the process was not an arbitration, but closer to an expert determination (see below). It is suggested that this approach is correct.

Chartered Society of Physiotherapy v Simmonds Church Smiles (1995)

The TCC judge in this case considered whether under the 1939 Act (the relevant terms of which are very similar to the 1996 Act) the surveyors carried out a statutory arbitration. He considered that there were some indications in the Act that it was an arbitration. For example, he thought the use in the Act of the words 'difference', 'settle' and 'award', and the provisions for decisions to be made by the surveyors, all suggested a judicial, or quasi-judicial, process. However, he thought that there were more indications to the contrary. For example, a party-appointed surveyor was obliged to retain his professional independence but not obliged to act without regard to the interests of the party who appointed him; there was no provision in the Act for a hearing or for the surveyors to proceed in a way expected of arbitrators; nor was there any obligation for the award to contain findings of fact or conclusions of law. He considered that an award under the Act was more in the nature of an expert determination than an arbitration award.

7.2 LIABILITY OF SURVEYORS

The question of whether party wall surveyors are arbitrators or not is important, as arbitrators (and adjudicators) are immune from liability.

Section 29, Arbitration Act 1996
Section 108(4), Housing Grants, Construction and
Regeneration Act 1996

Under these sections, arbitrators (or adjudicators) are not liable for anything done or omitted in the discharge or purported discharge of their functions as arbitrators (or adjudicators), unless the act or omission is shown to have been in bad faith.

The *Party Wall etc. Act* 1996 (although passed in the same year as the *Arbitration Act*) does not contain any provision dealing with the immunity of surveyors. Nor does it provide that the surveyors are to act as arbitrators. It is unlikely, in the light of *Chartered Society of Physiotherapy v Simmonds Church Smiles*, that party wall surveyors are arbitrators. They will therefore not have immunity under section 29 of the *Arbitration Act*.

It has been argued in a number of cases that experts, such as a valuer determining a rent review under a lease, are either arbitrators or 'quasi-arbitrators'. On this basis, it has been argued that they are immune from liability. However, the position is generally that experts do not act as arbitrators or quasi-arbitrators. (The definition of a quasi-arbitrator, if indeed such a person can exist, is far from clear from the cases. A quasi-arbitrator appears to be someone 'who is not quite an arbitrator' or is 'in much the same position as an arbitrator or judge'.) Experts are therefore not usually immune from liability.

Arenson v Casson Beckman Rutley & Co (1977)

Accountants were appointed to value shares at their fair value. The agreement stated that they would act as experts and not as arbitrators, but that their valuation would be final and binding on the parties. The plaintiff was unhappy with the valuation and sued the accountants for negligence. The issue was whether the accountants were immune, as they were acting in the position of arbitrators. Lord Wheatley set out some indications of circumstances in which a person would be immune:

(a) there was a dispute between the parties that had been formulated;

(b) the dispute had been remitted by the parties to the person in question to resolve in such a manner that he was called on to exercise a judicial function;

(c) where appropriate, the parties had been provided with an opportunity to present evidence and/or submissions in support of their respective claims in the dispute; and

(d) the parties had agreed to accept the decision of the person in question.

The House of Lords decided that the accountants in this case were not immune, as either arbitrators or quasi-arbitrators.

Palacath Ltd v Flanagan (1985)

A surveyor had been appointed to determine the rent under a rent review clause in a lease. The agreement stated that he was appointed to act as an expert and not an arbitrator. The plaintiff landlord was unhappy with the rent fixed by the surveyor. The issue arose of whether the surveyor had been appointed as a quasi-arbitrator and therefore had immunity from liability. The judge considered that the surveyor was not an arbitrator or quasi-arbitrator. In particular, the surveyor was entitled to rely on his own judgment and opinion; he was not limited in any way by the submissions of the parties; and he was not obliged to make any findings accepting or rejecting the parties' submissions. The judge therefore did not consider that he was acting in a judicial function and he was thus not entitled to immunity.

North Eastern Co-operative Society Ltd v Newcastle Upon Tyne City Council (1987)

The plaintiff and the defendant were parties to a lease. The rent review clause provided for the rent to be agreed by the parties and fixed by an independent surveyor agreed between them or by an arbitrator to be appointed by RICS. The defendant fixed the rent, having been appointed as the 'agreed surveyor'. The judge considered whether he had acted as an arbitrator or a quasi-arbitrator. He decided that the surveyor had not acted as an arbitrator. He was not prepared to decide that he was acting as a quasi-arbitrator, as he did not consider that any accurate meaning could be given to such an expression.

It therefore seems that party wall surveyors are likely to be liable for their acts or omissions in the carrying out of their functions under the 1996 Act. Party wall surveyors' liability might include, for example:

- the cost of remedial works if the party wall award authorises works that cause damage to the adjoining owner's property, for example, as a result of loss of or the inadequate replacement of support; and
- costs incurred by the parties if an award is invalid as a result of the surveyors exceeding their jurisdiction or proceeding without serving notices properly.

Brace v South East Regional Housing Association Ltd (1984)

The plaintiff and the first defendant, the Association, owned two terraced houses. The Association wished to demolish its house but not to rebuild it. Although the 1939 Act did not apply to the properties, the parties appointed surveyors and signed a party structure agreement. The agreement contained a schedule of permitted works. However, the demolition of the defendant's house caused the soil to dry out, as it was now open to the elements. The soil, which was clay, shrunk and caused subsidence damage to the plaintiff's house. The plaintiff claimed damages for negligence and the wrongful removal of support against both the Association and its surveyor. The defendants were not found negligent, but the judge held both defendants liable for wrongful removal of support. (The Court of Appeal dismissed the Association's appeal, but did not decide the appeal by the surveyor.)

Brace was not a case in which the surveyors were acting under one of the *Building Acts*. Where surveyors do not produce an award under the 1996 Act, there will be no question of immunity. The case does not therefore resolve the question of whether surveyors acting under the 1996 Act have immunity (as to which, see above). It does, however, illustrate a situation of potential liability for surveyors.

8
Remedies for failure to comply with the 1996 Act

Unfortunately, it is not uncommon for a building owner to do or propose work affecting a party wall which is not authorised by the *Party Wall etc. Act* 1996 and for which he does not have agreement or a party structure award. In such situations, the adjoining owner may wish to insist that the building owner complies with the 1996 Act before proceeding with the work. Alternatively, if the work has already been carried out and the adjoining owner has suffered damage, he will have claims at common law, for example, for nuisance, negligence, loss of support or trespass. In these cases, the adjoining owner has two main remedies:

- an injunction; or
- damages.

There are two types of injunction. **Prohibitory** (or quia timet) injunctions are Court orders preventing the building owner from commencing or continuing work. **Mandatory** injunctions are Court orders requiring the building owner to carry out a positive act, such as removing work that has already been carried out. Injunctions can be obtained either on an interim or a final basis. Interim injunctions (which were known as interlocutory injunctions prior to the introduction of the *Civil Procedure Rules* 1998) can be obtained quickly, particularly if the situation is urgent. Final injunctions are made at the final trial of a dispute.

8.1 INJUNCTIONS TO PREVENT WORK COMMENCING OR CONTINUING

In situations where the adjoining owner wishes to stop work proceeding without service of a notice under the 1996 Act or before the issue of an award, he is likely to seek an injunction. Where an urgent or quick solution to the problem of works commencing is needed, the application will need to be for an interim injunction.

Louis v Sadiq (1997)

The plaintiffs and defendant were neighbours whose properties were separated by a party wall. The defendant carried out significant demolition and rebuilding works to his house, which interfered with the party wall, causing damage to the plaintiffs' property. The defendant had not given notice as required by the *London Building Acts (Amendment) Act* 1939. The plaintiffs applied to Court for and obtained an interlocutory injunction. This order prevented the defendant from carrying out demolition or reconstruction works until he had complied with the Act. (The parties then had a dispute in relation to damages, which is the subject of the reported decision, referred to at 8.3 below.)

An adjoining owner may also wish to apply for an injunction to prevent work being carried out in accordance with a party wall award, where he considers that the award is invalid or has been made without jurisdiction.

Gyle-Thompson v Wall Street (Properties) Ltd (1974)

An award was made by two of the three surveyors that permitted the building owner to demolish and rebuild a party wall to a lesser height than its previous height. This was not permissible under the 1939 Act. The judge also found that the adjoining owners had not been properly served with the party wall notice and that their surveyor had not been properly appointed. For these reasons, the judge held that the award was invalid. The plaintiffs therefore obtained an injunction preventing the work from going ahead on the basis of the invalid party wall award.

8.2 INJUNCTIONS REQUIRING THE REMOVAL OF WORK ALREADY CARRIED OUT

If a building owner has already carried out work that was not authorised by the 1996 Act or was not done in accordance with the procedures in the Act, it will be too late to stop the work. On occasion, the adjoining owner may wish to apply for a mandatory injunction to force the building owner to remove the offending work. This may happen if, for example, the new work or building trespasses on to the adjoining owner's land.

It is extremely difficult to obtain a mandatory injunction at an interim stage. This is because, at an interim stage, unlike at a trial, not all the evidence is heard by the Court. If the Court orders a building owner to take down work that he has already built, and it turns out, after hearing all the evidence, that the building owner was right, the interim order will have caused injustice. The Court will therefore not grant an interim mandatory injunction unless it feels a high degree of assurance that the adjoining owner will be able to establish his right at trial.

London & Manchester Assurance Co Ltd v O & H Construction Ltd (1989)

The plaintiff and the defendant were the owners of adjoining wharves known as Albert and Albion Wharves in London. There was a party wall on the boundary of the sites. The defendant demolished this wall without first giving any notice to the plaintiff under the 1939 Act, and built new structures along the party wall line and within the plaintiff's site. The plaintiff claimed a mandatory injunction for the removal of the structures on the grounds of trespass and failure to comply with the 1939 Act. The judge, despite considering that making mandatory orders for removal of the structures at an interlocutory stage would be unusual, decided that it was justified in this case. He therefore gave injunctions for their removal on the basis both of trespass and failure to comply with the party wall procedures in the 1939 Act. He emphasised that the provisions of the *London Building Acts* were important and that the defendant, by tearing down a party wall and putting up its own wall instead, had acted in flagrant defiance of these provisions.

Whenever a party applies for an injunction, the Court considers whether to award damages instead, if damages would be an adequate remedy. This is because damages are seen as a less draconian remedy than an injunction.

Shelfer v City of London Electric Lighting Company (1895)

In this case, the Court of Appeal set out a working rule according to which a claimant will be awarded damages rather than an injunction, where the following requirements are met:

- the injury to the claimant's legal rights is small;
- the injury is capable of being estimated in money;
- the injury can be adequately compensated by a small money payment; and
- it would be oppressive to the defendant to grant an injunction.

Where the *Shelfer* requirements are not met, an injunction may be granted.

Daniells v Mendonca (1999)

The plaintiff and defendants owned adjoining properties. While the plaintiff was abroad, the defendants built an extension utilising a wall built entirely on the plaintiff's land, without her permission and without complying with the 1939 Act. The work was inadequate structurally and posed a fire risk. The plaintiff claimed a mandatory injunction requiring the removal of the part of the extension that encroached on her land and an order that the defendants should not carry out any further work without complying with the 1939 Act. She also claimed damages for trespass. The Court of Appeal decided that the original judge had been correct to grant a mandatory injunction for the removal of the encroachment. Although the trespass was only 1.5 inches over a length of 12 feet, the Court considered that the test in *Shelfer* had been satisfied. The Court did not think that the injury could be adequately compensated by a small payment. Nor did the Court consider that an injunction would be oppressive, relying, in particular, on the defendants' conduct, including their failure to comply with the 1939 Act.

8.3 DAMAGES

There will be situations in which an adjoining owner does not wish to claim an injunction. The adjoining owner may have suffered damage as a result of work that did not comply with the Act and may therefore wish to claim the cost of carrying out remedial works.

Roadrunner Properties Ltd v Dean and Suffolk and Essex (2004)

The building owner (the first defendant) had carried out work on its side of the party wall to form a chase for radiator pipes, without complying with the 1996 Act. The builder (the second defendant) had used a Kango hammer to form the chase. The adjoining owner claimed that damage had been caused by the defendants' works to its plasterwork and tiled floor. It was not entirely clear from the evidence that the works had caused the damage. However, the Court of Appeal considered that the lack of evidence was the defendants' fault for not complying with the Act (as no inspection of the wall by party wall surveyors had been possible prior to the works being carried out) and that the claimant had provided sufficient proof to succeed in its case.

On the other hand, an adjoining owner may have obtained or need an interim injunction to prevent further non-compliance with the 1996 Act, but also have suffered physical or financial damage as a result of the works carried out prior to the injunction. In such a situation, the adjoining owner will wish to claim damages in addition to an injunction. (As the building owner has not complied with the Act, the claim will be for damages at common law rather than compensation under section 7 of the 1996 Act.)

Louis v Sadiq (1997)

The plaintiffs and defendant were neighbours whose properties were separated by a party wall. The defendant carried out significant demolition and rebuilding works to his house, which interfered with the party wall, causing damage to the plaintiffs' property. The defendant had not given notice as required by the 1939 Act. The plaintiffs obtained an interlocutory injunction preventing further work without compliance with the Act. The defendant also repaired the physical damage. However, the plaintiffs claimed consequential damages, including costs incurred as a result of their inability to sell the property when they had planned, due to the defendant's works. The claim was for damages for nuisance. The Court of Appeal held that the defendant was liable at common law, in nuisance, as he had failed to comply with the Act.

8.4 REMEDIES FOR FAILURE TO COMPLY WITH AN AWARD

Remedies in situations where either of the owners fails or refuses to comply with an award are dealt with in 4.2 above.

9
Changes of ownership

9.1 INTRODUCTION

The *Party Wall etc.* Act 1996 contains specific provisions relating to situations that could arise in the future. For example:

- section 11(11) requires the adjoining owner to pay a proportion of the costs of the original works if he subsequently makes use of the works;
- section 1(3) contains a similar provision, that the expenses of a new party wall or party fence wall will be paid 'from time to time', depending on the use the parties make of the wall;
- section 11(10) allows an adjoining owner who has consented to special foundations to charge the other owner for any additional cost of the former's later building works caused by the presence of the special foundations.

By the time that the events identified in these sections arise, one or both of the properties may have been sold. The 1996 Act does not expressly provide for what happens in such situations (although, in relation to section 11(10), see 5.1.2 above).

The 1996 Act also does not provide for what happens if either the building owner or the adjoining owner sells the property either:

- after service of the notice but before the award; or
- after service of the award but before the works are completed.

9.2 REPAYMENT OF EXPENSES UNDER SECTION 11(11)

The 1996 Act does not make clear whether it is the original or the new building owner who should make a claim for repayment of expenses under this section, nor whether it is the original or the new adjoining owner who is liable to pay a contribution to the expenses of the original work. A limited number of cases have considered the question of claims for expenses under section 11(11) in relation to previous *Building Acts* with similar wording. The cases consider only the situation of the building owner, and not the adjoining owner. Unfortunately, clear principles do not emerge from the cases.

9.2.1 The position of the building owner

It seems that a subsequent tenant of the original building owner will not be able to recover expenses under this section from the adjoining owner. On the other hand, where the original building owner has sold the property before the adjoining owner starts to use the wall, it is the new building owner who is entitled to recover.

Re Stone and Hastie (1903)

A party wall had been raised by the freehold owners of Mr Hastie's property some years before he became a tenant of the property. Subsequently, the owner of the adjacent property, Mr Stone, wished to carry out works on the party wall. An award was made by surveyors which included a determination that Mr Stone should pay money to Mr Hastie to represent a proportion of the original costs of the works, as he was now making use of the party wall. Mr Hastie had not incurred the original costs (these had been incurred by the freehold owners). The Court of Appeal considered that this section allowed the recoupment of expenses only by the owner at whose expense the wall had been raised.

Mason v Fulham Corporation (1910)

The plaintiff wished to raise a party wall and served notice to that effect under the *London Building Act* 1894. He entered into an agreement with the defendant that, if and when the defendant subsequently wished to use the wall, the defendant would pay half of the expenses. This agreement was made to deal with the section of the 1894 Act that was equivalent to section 11(11) of the 1996 Act. By the time that the defendant wished to use the party wall, the plaintiff had sold his interest in the property. The plaintiff nonetheless tried to claim half of his expenses from the defendant. The Court decided that he was not entitled to any contribution, as the person entitled to the contribution under the Act was the person who was the building owner at the time when the money had to be paid (i.e., the plaintiff's successor in title). The rights to contribution had passed with the assignment of the property.

9.2.2 The position of the adjoining owner

Section 11(11) of the 1996 Act requires an adjoining owner who uses the work to pay a due proportion of the expenses of carrying out the work. Common sense would seem to dictate that it is the adjoining owner who actually wishes to use the wall (even if he was not involved at the time of the original party wall notice and works) who must contribute to the costs.

9.3 SALE BEFORE THE WORKS ARE COMPLETE

9.3.1 Sale by the building owner

If the building owner sells before the award is made, the most likely situation is that the proposed works will simply be abandoned.

However, there are potential problems in cases where the property is sold after an award has been made. The problem is only likely to apply if the works have not been properly or fully carried out. The question then is which building owner – the 'old' or the 'new' – will be required to comply with the award.

Selby v Whitbread & Co (1917)

The defendant served a notice under the 1894 Act, as he wished to demolish and rebuild his property (which adjoined the plaintiff's property). A party wall award was made in February 1915. The work carried out by the defendant involved setting the property back 13 ft from its previous position. The defendant sold the 13-ft area to the

London County Council in April 1915. The work was completed thereafter, but the plaintiff's wall was not properly supported, as a result of the setting back of the defendant's property. A second award was therefore made, requiring the defendant to support the plaintiff's property with a pier. The defendant did not do the work and the plaintiff made a claim in Court. The defendant argued (among a number of other points) that it was not obliged to comply with the award, as it had sold the land to the Council. This argument failed. The judge considered that the person who served the notice remained liable for all the results that followed from the notice and that the obligations were not transferred to the new owner of the land. He considered that if the argument were correct, it would seriously reduce the rights of adjoining owners, as it would enable a building owner, on discovering that the obligations under the award were more extensive than expected, to transfer the property to an owner without money and avoid its own obligations. He considered that *Mason v Fulham Corporation* related specifically to the sections of the Act considered (the recoupment of expenses) and that it related only to the assignment of a debt, not the assignment of obligations.

The logic of this approach can be understood. The case does not address the question (which is also not dealt with in the 1996 Act) of whether a new building owner would be bound by the award, in which he had no involvement. However, where work needs to be carried out from the new building owner's land, an order against the new building owner should ensure that support will actually be provided. An order that the original building owner pays damages will not necessarily enable the adjoining owner to have the work done. However, reliance on the *Access to Neighbouring Land Act* 1992 might be possible in a case involving loss of support (see 6.2 above).

9.3.2 Sale by the adjoining owner

If the award requires a contribution to be made by the adjoining owner to the cost of the works (for example, under section 11(4) of the 1996 Act), but the property is sold before the time for payment arises, it is not entirely clear whether the new or the original adjoining owner will be responsible. A fair result would appear to be payment by the original adjoining owner who was involved in the award. However, it has been indicated in *Carlish v Salt* (see below) that the liability would be that of the new adjoining owner.

Carlish v Salt (1906)

A party wall notice was served on the defendant, as adjoining owner, under the 1894 Act and an award made. The award allowed the building owner to carry out certain works, but directed that the adjoining owner should share the cost of the works when they were completed. The defendant (the adjoining owner) entered into a contract of sale with the plaintiff, who paid a deposit. The defendant did not inform the plaintiff about the party wall award. The plaintiff claimed return of his deposit. It was held that the existence of the party wall notice and award should have been disclosed to the intending purchaser, as it was a fact that materially affected the price to be paid, in so far as the notice and award imposed a liability of uncertain amount on the owner of the premises.

There have been no decisions on the question of whether an adjoining owner would be obliged effectively to put up with works carried out pursuant to a notice or an award served on the previous owner.

9.4   REGISTRATION OF RIGHTS AGAINST LAND

It is possible, in certain circumstances, to register charges against land that bind subsequent purchasers of land or allow the person registering the charge to be given notice prior to any dealings with the land. For example, section 4 of the *Access to Neighbouring Land Act* 1992 allows registration of an access order against the other owner's land. This binds subsequent purchasers. The 1996 Act, on the other hand, does not expressly provide that any rights under it or awards can be registered.

It has now been decided that a party wall award does not entitle an adjoining owner to register a caution against the building owner's land. (A caution can be registered against land in order to prevent dealings with it without notice being given to the person who registered the caution. However, in order to be entitled to register a caution, a party must have an interest in the land.)

Observatory Hill Ltd v Camtel Investments SA (1997)

A party wall award entitled the plaintiff (the building owner) to carry out work. It imposed on the plaintiff an obligation to make good damage to the defendant's building and provided that, if he failed to do so, the adjoining owner was entitled to carry out such works at the plaintiff's expense and on the plaintiff's land. The works caused damage to the defendant's land and the defendant registered a caution against the land at the Land Registry. The plaintiff applied to Court to have the caution removed. The defendant argued that it had a sufficient interest in the land to register a caution, as the award:

(a) permitted the work to be carried out on land partly the property of each party;

(b) required the plaintiff to make good damage at its own expense to the defendant's building; and

(c) entitled the defendant to enter the plaintiff's land to carry out making good at the plaintiff's expense, if the latter failed to do so.

The judge decided that an adjoining owner with the benefit of an award under the *London Building Acts (Amendment) Act 1939* did not have a sufficient interest in the land to be entitled to register a caution.

10
The common law of support
– traditional and modern –
and the 1996 Act

10.1 THE TRADITIONAL COMMON LAW OF RIGHTS AND EASEMENTS OF SUPPORT

Land and buildings, in certain circumstances, have rights to be supported by adjacent or subjacent land or buildings. These rights form part of the common law. There are two types of rights of support – a natural right of support and an easement of support.

10.1.1 Right of support of land by land – the 'natural right of support'

Land has what is known as a 'natural right of support' from adjacent land. This is not an 'easement of support' (which can be acquired in a number of ways – see 10.1.2 below). It simply naturally arises out of the ownership of land. The existence of the natural right of support means that the owner of land A cannot remove the support from adjacent land B so as to cause damage to land B. This is the case whether land A supports land B vertically or laterally.

Davis v Treharne (1881)

It was held in this case that the person who owns the surface of the land has a right to have it properly supported below by minerals. If minerals below the surface are being mined, proper support for the land must be provided, in place of the minerals extracted.

The natural right of support gives land – but not buildings – a right of support from adjacent land. However, if work on land A removes support from land B, causing damage to the land and consequent damage to a building, the owner of land B could claim for the damage to the building, as well as to the land.

Ray v Fairway Motors (Barnstaple) Ltd (1968)

The plaintiff and defendant owned adjoining properties separated by a wall owned by the plaintiff. The plaintiff had built a workshop against the wall. The defendant excavated adjacent to the wall and, shortly afterwards, the plaintiff's wall cracked and began to bulge, causing damage to the workshop. The plaintiff claimed damages for interference with the natural right of support, an easement of support and negligence. The Court of Appeal decided that the plaintiff could not succeed in a claim for breach of the natural right of support. He could not show sufficient damage to the land, as opposed to damage to the building, in order to have a claim for breach of the natural right of support. If he could have shown damage to the land, he could have claimed for the consequential damage to the building. (He did, however, succeed in a claim for breach of an easement.)

The natural right of support relates to support by the soil (minerals) and not support by underground water. This means that the natural right of support does not prevent owner A from draining water from the soil and thereby causing damage or subsidence to the adjacent land of owner B.

Popplewell v Hodkinson (1869)

The plaintiff owned marshy land on which he had built cottages. The adjacent land was owned by trustees who employed the defendant to build a church on their land. The defendant's excavations for the church caused the plaintiff's land to be drained. The land subsided and the cottages suffered from subsidence damage. On appeal, the Court decided that, although it was not permissible for an owner to withdraw the support of adjacent soil [i.e., there was a natural right of support], there was nothing to prevent the owner from draining the soil. The plaintiff's claim therefore failed.

Langbrook Properties Ltd v Surrey County Council (1970)

The plaintiffs were property developers building a development of shops, offices and residential accommodation. The defendant was responsible for excavations on the adjacent land for the construction of the M3. In order to keep the excavations dry, water had to be pumped out. The plaintiffs claimed that this had led to removal of water from beneath their land and caused the buildings on their land to settle. The judge decided that, as a matter of principle, a person could abstract water that ran in undefined channels under his land, even if this resulted in the removal of water under his neighbour's land and caused damage to that land. The plaintiff's claim, which was for nuisance and negligence, therefore failed.

Stephens v Anglian Water Authority (1987)

The plaintiff was the owner of a cottage. She claimed that subsidence had been caused to her cottage by the negligence of the defendant water authority in extracting large volumes of water from the land. The Court of Appeal decided that an owner of land had a right to abstract subterranean water flowing in undefined channels beneath his land, regardless of the consequences for his neighbour's land. The plaintiff therefore had no claim in negligence.

The principle set out in the above cases could be very unfair on the innocent adjacent owner who has been deprived of the support of his land. As a result, it has been narrowly applied, so that it applies only to water and not, for example, to silt or brine.

Trinidad Asphalt Company v Ambard (1899)

The defendant's business involved excavating a stratum of asphalt or pitch on its ground. Once pitch is excavated and exposed to the atmosphere, it melts and oozes out. The defendant's excavation went up to the boundary of the plaintiff's land and, as a result, pitch oozed out of the plaintiff's land and caused damage by removing its support. It was argued that the plaintiff had no claim on the basis of the principle relating to water. However, the Privy Council decided that, although pitch became liquid once exposed, it was a mineral and not water. The plaintiff therefore had a right of support and succeeded in its claim.

Jordeson v Sutton, Southcoates and Drypool Gas Company (1899)

The plaintiff owned land with houses on it. The defendant, in the course of excavations for the construction of a gasometer on its adjacent land, dug into an underground stratum of quicksand or 'running silt', which ran under both parties' land. The defendant removed silt and pumped out the water from its land, in the process causing subsidence to the plaintiff's land and houses. The defendant argued that the plaintiff had no claim, as the subsidence had been caused by the removal of water. The Court of Appeal decided that the plaintiff's house was supported, not by water, but by a bed of wet sand or running silt. The plaintiff's right of support had therefore been infringed and he was entitled to succeed in his claim.

Lotus Ltd v British Soda Co Ltd (1972)

The defendant's business involved the extraction of wild brine from salt beds beneath its land. This operation involved the saturation of the rock salt beneath the land and its extraction by pumping. The works caused subsidence to the plaintiff's land and factory. The judge decided that the principle relating to water was not applicable to an operation that consisted of causing a solid support, the salt beds, to liquefy, and then removing the resulting liquid. The plaintiff therefore had a right of support from the minerals beneath the land and succeeded in its claim.

Brace v South East Regional Housing Association Ltd (1984)

This case concerned an easement of support, rather than the natural right of support. However, arguments about support by water were raised. The plaintiff and the defendant owned two terraced houses. The defendant demolished its house and did not rebuild it. The demolition of the defendant's house caused the soil to dry out, as it was now open to the elements. The soil, which was clay, shrunk, and caused subsidence damage to the plaintiff's house. The plaintiff claimed damages for wrongful removal of support. The defendant argued that the damage had been caused by the removal of underground water (i.e., from the clay); that the plaintiff had no right of support from water; and that the claim must therefore fail. The Court of Appeal disagreed. The damage had, in fact, been caused by altering the conditions that operated to provide support, and thereby allowing the soil to dry out, rather than by draining off water. The principle relating to water therefore did not provide a defence to the plaintiff's claim.

10.1.2 Right of support of buildings by land and by other buildings – easements of support

The natural right of support applies primarily to support provided to the land by other land. Buildings, however, can acquire a right of support, known as an easement of support, from other land or from other buildings.

10.1.2.1 Acquisition of an easement of support

An easement of support is acquired either by prescription or by grant.

Prescription

The doctrine of prescription allows a party who has made use of support from other land or buildings for a period of 20 years to acquire an easement of support after that period. The main ways in which a prescriptive right can be acquired are under the *Prescription Act* 1832 or under a doctrine called 'lost modern grant'.

Dalton v Angus (1881)

Two owners had built houses at the edge of their property, although the houses were not terraced. The plaintiff had converted the house on its land to a coach factory. This involved removing the internal walls so that more support was required from the adjacent soil than had previously been the case. More than 20 years after this, the defendant demolished the house on its land and excavated the land. This deprived the factory of the necessary lateral support from the soil, and it collapsed. The House of Lords decided that the plaintiff had acquired a right of support for its coach factory from the defendant's land, by prescription, as a result of the 20 years' use of the soil for support. The defendant was therefore liable to pay damages for removal of the support.

Lemaitre v Davis (1881)

The plaintiff and the defendant owned terraced properties. The defendant employed a contractor to demolish his property. The demolition was carried out without shoring up or otherwise supporting the plaintiff's property and damage was caused. The judge decided that an easement of support could be acquired by a building from another building by prescription under the *Prescription Act* 1832. It was held that both the contractor and the defendant owner were liable for the removal of support.

Grant

An easement can be expressly granted in the conveyance of property or in another agreement between the owners. The grant of an easement can also be implied into conveyances under a doctrine known as 'the rule in *Wheeldon v Burrows*' and under section 62 of the *Law of Property Act* 1925. The basis for both these methods of implication is, essentially, that although the rights have not been mentioned in the conveyance, they were used or enjoyed prior to the conveyance.

Byard v Co-operative Permanent Building Society Ltd (1970)

The plaintiff and the defendant owned terraced properties. There was an express grant of an easement of support. They entered into an agreement in a deed relating to the carrying out of works of demolition and rebuilding which provided that the defendant granted to the plaintiff 'full right of support for the first building and any other building which may hereafter be erected on the site'.

Bradburn v Lindsay (1983)

The plaintiff and the defendant each owned a semi-detached house, separated by a party wall. The defendant conceded that the plaintiff's property had a right of support from the defendant's property on the basis of the principle in *Wheeldon v Burrows*.

10.1.2.2 What is a right of support for buildings?

The right of support that one building has from another is not simply a right to support the weight of the building. It includes a right to 'wind support' – that is, support against the effects of the wind.

Rees v Skerrett (2001)

The plaintiff and defendant owned adjoining terraced houses separated by a party wall. The defendant was served with notices by the local authority which required him to demolish his building and shore up and weatherproof the adjoining building. The defendant carried out the demolition works but failed to provide adequate shoring or protection for the exposed wall. As a result of the removal of lateral support, the plaintiff's property was damaged by suction damage when the wind blew along the front of the property or along the exposed flank wall. The judge decided that the plaintiff was owed a right of support, but that this right did not include a right to 'wind support'. The Court of Appeal disagreed, deciding that 'wind support' was one aspect of the right of support that one adjoining building has from another. The plaintiff's claim for interference with his easement of support therefore succeeded.

10.1.3 The extent of the landowner's duties under the traditional law

There are three key points that define the extent of the rights and obligations of the parties where there is either a natural right of support or an easement of support.

10.1.3.1 Landowner has no duty to take active steps to maintain support

The owner of the land that provides the support may not take positive steps to remove the support without providing equivalent support. However, he does not have a duty to take any active steps to maintain or repair his own property so as to maintain the support.

Sack v Jones (1925)

The plaintiff and defendant owned adjoining terraced properties with mutual easements of support. The plaintiff's house suffered from cracking and other structural damage. She alleged that this was caused by the defendant's house pulling her house over, as a result of lack of repair. The plaintiff failed to prove this on the facts. However, the judge decided that even if she had succeeded on the facts, she would have had no claim for breach of the easement of support. The defendant was, as a result of the easement of support, under no obligation to keep her house in repair in order to provide support to the plaintiff's property.

Bond v Nottingham Corporation (1940)

In this case, the Court of Appeal set out the principle, applicable in cases of easements of support, that the owner of the building providing the support is under no obligation to repair that part of the building that provides support for his neighbour. He can let it fall into decay. If it does fall into decay and support is removed, the owner of the dominant tenement has no cause for complaint. On the other hand, the owner of the building that provides support is not entitled, by a positive act, to remove support without providing equivalent support.

10.1.3.2 **Landowner is liable without negligence**

An owner of land who removes support from the adjacent land can be liable even if his actions were not negligent.

Brace v South East Regional Housing Association Ltd (1984)

The plaintiff and the Association owned two adjoining terraced houses. The Association wished to demolish its house and did not intend to rebuild it. The *London Building Acts (Amendment) Act* 1939 did not apply to the properties, although the parties appointed surveyors and signed a party structure agreement. Despite the fact that the works carried out were agreed, the demolition of the defendant's house caused damage to the plaintiff's house, as a result of shrinkage of the clay soil. The plaintiff claimed damages for negligence and wrongful removal of support. The plaintiff's property had acquired a right of support from the defendant's property by prescription. The judge found that the defendant was not negligent, but was liable for the removal of support. The Court of Appeal upheld the finding that the defendant was liable for wrongful removal of support, as support had been removed and adequate alternative support had not been provided.

If a defendant is sued in tort for negligence, he can usually successfully defend an action on the basis that he fulfilled his duty of care by engaging a competent independent contractor. However, there are exceptions to this general rule, one of which is cases of withdrawal of support. In such cases, the owner is liable even where the works that result in the loss of support are undertaken by an independent contractor.

Bower v Peate (1876)

The plaintiff and the defendant were owners of adjoining houses. The defendant pulled down his house, intending to rebuild it. These works involved the excavation and removal of soil that had supported the plaintiff's house, and also required underpinning. The defendant engaged a builder to carry out the works. The plaintiff's house suffered damage as a result of defective underpinning and lack of support. The defendant argued that he was not liable, as he had engaged a contractor to carry out the works. It was held that the defendant was liable. The Court stated that:

> 'a man who orders a work to be executed, from which, in the natural course of things, injurious consequences to his neighbour must be expected to arise, unless means are adopted by which such consequences may be prevented, is bound to see to the doing of that which is necessary to prevent the mischief, and cannot relieve himself of his responsibility by employing someone else...to do what is necessary to prevent the act he has ordered to be done from becoming wrongful.'

10.1.3.3 Landowner has no liability for natural phenomena

If the support is removed by a natural phenomenon, the owner of the property providing support will not be liable.

Rouse v Gravelworks Ltd (1940)

The plaintiff owned farmland adjacent to the defendant's gravel quarry. The defendant excavated his land to remove the gravel. The area excavated filled up with rainwater and formed a pond. As a result of the action of the water in the pond, and the wind, the plaintiff's adjacent bank was eroded and undermined. The plaintiff claimed damages for withdrawal of support. The Court of Appeal held that there was no cause of action, as the defendant was entitled to carry out the excavation, and any loss of support was the result not of direct action by the defendant, but of the natural action of the elements.

10.2 THE UNSATISFACTORY STATE OF THE TRADITIONAL LAW

The traditional law on rights and easements of support is not entirely satisfactory, when viewed from the standpoint of the adjacent landowner. There are a number of obvious problems, including the following.

- A right of support of one building from another, or from land, has to be acquired. Unless there is an express or implied grant of such a right, it takes 20 years to acquire this right (by prescription). In the first 20 years, therefore, in such cases, a building owner can remove his building without being liable for interference with an easement of support.
- Even where a right has been acquired, the owner of the land is only liable if he actively removes support, and not if he fails to take active steps to maintain support. However, the active removal of support and the failure to maintain support can both have the same effect on the adjacent land or property.
- A building owner cannot remove the support of the soil from his neighbour's land, but he can drain water from the land. Both of these activities could have the same effect on the adjacent land.

10.3. THE MODERN LAW

10.3.1 The effect of the 1996 Act on the traditional law

The 1939 Act applied only to London. Its effect on rights and duties of support was therefore limited to works in London. The 1996 Act, however, extended the principles to the whole country. As a result of this, although the 1996 Act did not set out to reform the law on rights and easements of support, it seems to have had that effect.

Section 2 of the 1996 Act

Section 2 of the 1996 Act does not specifically deal with issues of support. However, although there is no positive duty in section 2 to provide alternative support when carrying out works that affect the party wall, awards will and should provide for alternative support where necessary. There is no need for an adjoining owner to demonstrate that he has an easement of support at common law, in order to be entitled to support in relation to works carried out under the Act. The adjoining owner will, as a result of the Act and the award, be entitled to the provision of adequate alternative support if the proposed works remove support.

Selby v Whitbread & Co (1917)

The defendant demolished and rebuilt his property further back than its previous position, leaving the front of the flank wall of the plaintiff's property inadequately supported. A party wall award was made, requiring the defendant to provide a pier to support the front part of the plaintiff's wall. This award was enforced by the Court.

Section 6 of the 1996 Act

It is now necessary, in certain instances covered by section 6 of the Act, for a building owner who wishes to excavate on his own land to give notice if such excavation is within six metres of the adjacent owner's building or structure. Having given notice, he is then required, if necessary, to carry out works to safeguard the adjoining owner's foundations (section 6(3)).

Therefore, for excavations at the depths and within the distances provided for in section 6 of the 1996 Act, some of the problems with the traditional law have been removed. In section 6 cases, it will no longer matter whether the result of the excavation is to remove the support of the soil or water. In any such case where support is required, the building owner will be obliged to provide support.

10.3.2 **The effect of the new law of measured duties of care on the traditional law**

In addition to the 1996 Act, the problems with the traditional law of support have been reduced by recent developments in the law of nuisance and negligence. The law of nuisance and negligence now provides that a landowner may owe his neighbour a 'measured duty of care'. This measured duty of care may require an owner to take positive steps to prevent foreseeable damage to an adjoining property. Therefore, where an owner simply lets his land or building fall into disrepair, rather than actively withdrawing support, he may now be liable in nuisance or negligence for breach of a measured duty of care.

Bradburn v Lindsay (1983)

The 'new law' of support began to be fully developed by the Court of Appeal in *Holbeck Hall* in 2000 (see below). However, *Bradburn v Lindsay* (referred to in *Holbeck Hall*) could be considered to be the true starting point for the new law. The plaintiff and the defendant each owned a semi-detached house, separated by a party wall. The defendant allowed her property to fall into disrepair. It was dilapidated and suffering from dry rot. The plaintiff complained to the defendant and the council. The council eventually demolished the property. This left the plaintiff's property without adequate support and the plaintiff claimed damages for nuisance and negligence. The defendant argued that although an owner was not entitled actively to remove support from an adjacent property without providing equivalent support, there was no duty to maintain a property in good repair so that it continued to provide support. The judge decided that the defendant owed the plaintiff a duty to take reasonable steps to prevent damage being caused by the lack of repair of her property. She was therefore liable to the plaintiff for damages for the loss of support.

Holbeck Hall Hotel Ltd v Scarborough Borough Council (2000)

The plaintiffs were the owners and lessees of a hotel and grounds at the top of a cliff. The defendant council owned the land between the hotel grounds and the sea. The cliff was subject to marine erosion and the cliff slopes were inherently unstable and subject to local slips. In 1993 a massive land slip caused loss of support to the hotel grounds and part of the hotel. The hotel had to be demolished. The land slip was caused by natural causes and not by any positive act of the defendant. It was argued by the defendant that it could only be liable if it had taken active steps to remove support, which it had not, and that there was no positive duty to provide support or keep the cliff in a condition where it continued to support the hotel and grounds. The Court of Appeal, however, disagreed, deciding that the defendant owed the plaintiffs a measured duty of care to prevent damage to the plaintiffs' land due to natural causes. The duty arises, according to the Court of Appeal, in relation to a patent defect of which the defendant knew or ought to have known. The duty is limited. It requires the landowner to do what is reasonable in the circumstances to prevent or minimise the risk. In determining whether the duty has been breached, the Court can consider how practicable it is to prevent or minimise damage, how difficult or expensive measures would be, the amount of time available and the ability of the defendant to carry out such measures. On the facts of this case, the Court of Appeal decided that the defendant was not in breach of the duty. The defendant had foreseen the danger of slips, but not a slip of this magnitude. The full extent of the defect was latent and the defendant was not liable.

As the measured duty of care (which has been called 'reasonableness between neighbours' by the Court of Appeal) is limited to a requirement to do what is reasonable in the circumstances, this does not mean that a defendant who owes such a duty will always be obliged to pay for all damage suffered by the other property.

Abbahall Ltd v Smee (2003)

This case did not concern loss of support, but it dealt with the question of damages where a measured duty of care was owed. The defendant, the owner of the first and second floors and roof of a block of flats, had allowed the roof of the flats to fall into disrepair. The Court of Appeal found that she owed a measured duty of care to the plaintiff, the owner of the ground floor flat. The Court of Appeal decided that where there was a measured duty of care, a Court's decision as to who paid the costs of repair would depend on what was fair, just and reasonable in the circumstances and what was reasonable between neighbours. In the circumstances of the case, the Court of Appeal decided that the plaintiff and the defendant should each pay for half of the remedial costs.

10.3.3 The current relevance of the law of easements and rights of support

In the light of the 1996 Act and the new 'measured duty of care', the difficulties with the law on easements and rights of support have been reduced. However, there still remain situations in which the law on easements and rights of support may be important. The following examples illustrate this.

■ Work done without compliance with the 1996 Act

A building owner who carries out work without giving the notices required by the 1996 Act may be liable for interference with a party's rights of support, as well as in nuisance and negligence. This is dealt with in Chapter 8 above.

■ Excavations not covered by section 6 of the 1996 Act

Section 6 of the 1996 Act identifies situations in which notice must be served on adjoining owners, and their foundations protected, if necessary. It remains possible for excavations that do not fall within the notice provisions of section 6 to cause damage to adjacent premises. In such situations, the excavating owner may be liable for interference with a right or easement of support, as well as in negligence or nuisance.

■ Claims against the contractor

The 1996 Act places duties on the building owner. However, an adjoining owner who suffers damage may wish to sue the contractor who carried out the work, rather than the building owner. This could occur, for example, if the building owner had no money and would therefore not be able to meet any judgment against him. A claim against a contractor would still need to be made on the basis of the law in relation to interference with rights of support, nuisance or negligence.

- **Work carried out in accordance with a party wall award but which still interferes with an easement of support**

It is unfortunately possible for a building owner to carry out work to a party wall in accordance with a party wall award, but for damage still to be caused to the adjacent property as a result of loss of support. In such a case it seems likely, although it has yet to be decided by the Courts, that the adjoining owner's claim against the building owner would be for compensation under section 7(2) of the 1996 Act and not for interference with an easement of support (see 6.1.3.1 above). A claim against the party wall surveyors, on the other hand, would still be made relying on common law rights. Such claims could include interference with an easement of support, negligence or nuisance.

Brace v South East Regional Housing Association Ltd (1984)

The plaintiff and the Association owned adjoining houses. The Association wished to demolish its house and did not intend to rebuild it. The 1939 Act did not apply to the properties, although the parties appointed surveyors and signed a party structure agreement. The agreement contained a schedule of permitted works. Despite the fact that the works carried out were agreed, the demolition of the defendant's house caused damage to the plaintiff's house, as a result of shrinkage of the clay soil. The plaintiff claimed damages for negligence and wrongful removal of support against the Association's surveyor, as well as against the Association. The Association and the surveyor were not found to be negligent, but the claim for wrongful removal of support succeeded against them. The claim against the Association was upheld in the Court of Appeal. (The claim against the surveyor was not decided on the appeal.)

Index

Index

The Case in Point Series

The *Case in Point* series is an exciting new set of concise practical guides to legal issues in land, property and construction. Written for the property professional, they get straight to the key issues in a refreshingly jargon-free style

Areas covered:

Negligence in Valuation and Surveys
Stock Code: 6388
Published: December 2002

Service Charges
Due for publication: June 2004

Estate Agency
Due for publication: July 2004

Lease Renewal
Due for publication: January 2005

Rent Review
Due for publication: January 2005

Construction Adjudication
Due for publication: February 2005

If you would like to be kept informed when new *Case in Point* titles are published, please e-mail rbmarketing@rics.org.uk

How to order:

All RICS Books titles can be ordered direct by:

☎ Telephoning 0870 333 1600 (Option 3)
🖰 Online at www.ricsbooks.com
🖷 E-mail mailorder@rics.org.uk